BRITAIN'S BEST POLITICAL CARTOONS 2016

Dr Tim Benson is Britain's leading authority on political cartoons. He runs The Political Cartoon Gallery and Café which is located near the River Thames in Putney. He has produced numerous books on political cartoonists, including *Churchill in Caricature, Low and the Dictators, The Cartoon Century: Modern Britain through the Eyes of Its Cartoonists, Drawing the Curtain: The Cold War in Cartoons* and *Over the Top: A Cartoon History of Australia at War.*

BRITAIN'S BEST POLITICAL CARTOONS 2016

Edited by Tim Benson

BOOKS

3 5 7 9 10 8 6 4 2

Random House Books
20 Vauxhall Bridge Road
London SW1V 2SA

Random House Books is part of the Penguin Random House
group of companies whose addresses can be found
at global.penguinrandomhouse.com

Penguin
Random House
UK

First published by Random House Books in 2016

www.penguin.co.uk

A CIP catalogue record for this book is available from the British Library

ISBN 9781847947932

Typeset in 11/15.5 pt Amasis MT Light by Jouve (UK), Milton Keynes

Printed and bound in Italy by LEGO, S.p.A.

Penguin Random House is committed to a sustainable future
for our business, our readers and our planet. This book is made from
Forest Stewardship Council® certified paper

MIX
Paper from
responsible sources
FSC® C018179

INTRODUCTION

Why is it that political cartoonists in Britain tend to focus far more on the American presidential race than on the general elections of any other country? One obvious reason is that we share a common language, enjoy cultural similarities and have an intertwined history with the United States. Remember the old adage, 'When America sneezes, Britain catches a cold'? Cartoonists appreciate that whoever the American people elect as their president has a significant impact on us in the UK. According to the cartoonist Brian Adcock: 'Some people think that not being American and not having a vote means that we should also not have a view on who becomes their next president, a notion that I thoroughly disagree with. I only need refer their attention to American foreign policy during recent decades to show that whoever the American people choose to be their commander-in-chief affects us all.' However, not all cartoonists feel this way. Peter Brookes has stated that he is only interested in American politics when it directly impinges on us in Britain, such as when

THE WEST WEIGHS UP.

Sir Bernard Partridge's take on the 1944 American presidential election, in which incumbent Democrat Franklin D. Roosevelt defeated the Republican Thomas E. Dewey, appeared in *Punch* on 8 November 1944.

Blair and Bush decided to depose Saddam. 'To me, the presidential elections are a sideshow compared to what's going on over here,' he says.

And yet, American politics continues to have a significant influence on how we conduct things in the UK. British party leaders try to appear presidential in style (Jeremy Corbyn being a current exception to the rule) – presentation is all-important, and looking good on television and on social media is just as vital here as it is in the States. Appearing presidential, or indeed prime ministerial, is crucial to gaining power. According to Ben Jennings: 'Our own elections have become more focused on the personality and image of the leader, as it is in the United States. This is why Ed Miliband was doomed from the start, whereas David Cameron looked like the guy you'd get to play a British prime minister in a film.'

Party conferences in the UK have also become slicker and are now meticulously stage-managed. Dissent is not tolerated, and long ovations for speeches by the prime minister and the party leaders are the norm. Until the 1980s, Labour party conferences in particular were often free-for-alls, complete with booing, heckling and barracking. Peter Hitchens remembers 'howls of rage, walk-outs and factional baying at Labour conferences, along with genuinely contested elections for office,

and even some acerbity over the European Union at Tory ones. These days, even the fringe meetings are uncontroversial and worthy.' Now, like American conventions, British party conferences are generally demonstrations of unity and decorum.

However, a fundamental difference between British and American elections is the length of the campaigns; the former usually take place over a period of just one month, while the latter lasts almost a year. According to American cartoonist Kevin Kallaugher: 'British elections are defined by their intense brevity. Over a course of a few weeks there is a bluster of political bombast. By contrast, the US election is a marathon to the UK's sprint. The sheer size of the United States means months and months of campaigning, dozens of candidate debates and thousands of hours of TV ads. For the US cartoonist, this is a double-edged sword. The campaign engages the readers at the same time as it bores and annoys them.'

Another major difference is that, prior to their epic campaign, American presidential candidates have not faced anything like the rigour that British political leaders have. Imagine Ronald Reagan, George W. Bush, Dan Quayle, Donald Trump or Sarah Palin negotiating Prime Minister's Question Time, let alone performing sufficiently well as a parliamentarian to be chosen as a party leader. This is probably one reason why gaffe-prone presidential hopefuls have over the years represented such great material for cartoonists: in British politics, the best climb to the top of the greasy pole over time, which gives both the cartoonists and the public the opportunity to get to know them. By contrast, when a little-known governor, congressman or senator runs for the White House and is thrust into the political spotlight, it can catch the cartoonists off guard, leaving them unable to capture what David Low called a politician's 'inner essence'. In the past, cartoonists would sometimes label unknown politicians so the reader knew who they were, but this is a practice that most British cartoonists avoid. Christian Adams says: 'It's crass to label people. If I think the reader won't recognise a political figure, then I won't draw him or her. That's why I haven't drawn Bernie Sanders – very few people in Britain would know who he is.' However, in the States, labelling hasn't been necessary in this electoral cycle. According to Kallaugher: 'The most important feature of the US campaign is that often most Americans do not know the candidates well before a campaign starts. This year has been an exception – most folks already had an opinion of Hillary Clinton and Donald Trump.'

America has a long tradition of animals symbolising their political parties, something that we in Britain lack. Though we have the Labour rose, the Lib Dem bird and the Conservative tree (formerly a torch), motifs which are used occasionally by cartoonists, they do not have the same recognition factor as the Republican elephant or the Democratic donkey, which the Democrat party appropriated as far back as the early nineteenth century. During the presidential election of 1828, the Democrat candidate Andrew Jackson was labelled a 'jackass' by his opponents. Amused by the slur, he decided to use it to his own advantage, putting a donkey on his campaign posters and pointing out the animal's persistence, loyalty and the ability to carry a heavy load. The donkey also symbolised humble origins and simplistic virtues, which helped Jackson further differentiate himself from his aristocratic Republican opponent, John Quincy Adams.

However, it was actually the great nineteenth-century American cartoonist Thomas Nast who made the donkey the symbol of the Democrats. Nast drew the animal, which was originally supposed to represent an anti-Civil War faction of the party, for the first time in an 1870 cartoon for *Harper's Weekly*. The donkey caught the public's imagination, and by 1880 it had become the party's

For nearly 150 years, the Republican and Democratic parties have been represented in cartoons as an elephant and donkey.

unofficial symbol. Nast was also responsible for the creation of the Republican elephant. In a cartoon that also appeared in *Harper's Weekly* in 1874, he drew a donkey disguised in lion's skin, scaring away all the animals at the zoo. One of those animals, the elephant, was labelled 'The Republican Vote'. From that moment, the elephant became synonymous with the Republican party. These symbols still remain popular with American cartoonists, sometimes even to the neglect of the politicians themselves, according to Vicky: 'American cartoonists put everything into the mouths of their symbols without much bothering about the human personalities who really run the parties.'

While British cartoonists are often keen to cover the elections of other countries, their editors are sometimes less enthusiastic. According to Bob Moran: 'It's often difficult to persuade editors that a cartoon about America is important. There needs to be very little happening domestically, and the cartoon has to be especially well-conceived. Another difficulty is that the US political system is quite alien to most British people, so anything you do has to be fairly broad.' Peter Brookes feels the sheer geographical distance between the two countries and the different traditions and sensibilities deters him from commenting on American politics: 'Covering American elections,' he says, 'is a bit like American cartoonists trying to cover British ones – they invariably get it all wrong.' Andy Davey has found that some editors he has worked for border on the xenophobic: 'No editor would let you bang on about the French/ Belgian/Nigerian/Egyptian/Mexican elections, unless several hundred people had been massacred at a polling station or a llama had been elected president. I did manage to do a cartoon about the Afghan elections for the *Sun* once, but this is less surprising than it sounds – the editorial staff were keen to show how successful the interminable British entanglement in Afghanistan had been in bringing "democracy" to the country.' Davey also believes that because UK readers are unable to vote in the US, newspaper proprietors have less interest in the presidential elections because they cannot affect the outcome.

Despite a good deal of British cartoonists being keen to comment upon US presidential elections, the enthusuiasm is not always reciprocated by their American colleagues. As Kallaugher explains: 'Despite being "The Leader of the Free World", in reality we're incredibly provincial. Most Americans do not even know the name of their own vice president, let alone the prime minister of Great Britain. If they did recognise David Cameron, they'd assume he resided in Downton Abbey. Perhaps if Theresa May threatened to nuke Budweiser for insulting the good name of beer, Americans might stand up and take notice!'

Furthermore, unlike British prime ministers, presidents of the United States are also heads of state, and so prime minister and monarch combined. According to David Low: 'The president is of the people but, by virtue of his office, a being apart. Although the president's public character is that of the "ordinary man", the journey is as royal a

progress as could be compatible with popular democracy.' As a consequence, American cartoonists appear to show some degree of deference to their president, even while satirising them. British cartoonists feel no such constraints and treat the president as they do any other political figure. It was no surprise that when Steve Bell depicted George W. Bush as a stupid, apelike creature, he upset many Americans. Bob Moran also found himself in hot water when he visited the United States: 'I think there is a fascination with the contrast between how little reverence we bestow on our politicians in Britain compared to the huge evangelical rallies witnessed during US campaigns. I went to see some publications in New York with my portfolio. One of the cartoons inside was of then president George W. Bush as a baby in a nappy using the American flag as a playmat. It didn't go down well at all – I remember being surprised at how offensive people found it. I think British cartoonists enjoy the idea that they can portray American politicians in ways that American cartoonists are not permitted to.' American newspaper editors tend to be far more prudish about what cartoonists can get away with – they feel their readers would never tolerate nudity, bad language or anything that would denigrate the presidency.

Since the founding of *Punch* in 1841, British cartoonists have regularly commented on presidential elections. The first British cartoonist to visit the United States during an election was David Low in 1936. While in Washington D. C., Low was invited to the White House to draw President Roosevelt. According to Low, Roosevelt was 'a bad sitter. From the waist up alive and on the move all the time, ruffling his hair, throwing his arms about, twisting his body, turning his face to the ceiling, laughing too much, either opening his mouth or distorting its shape by wedging his cigarette holder too far to the side. He might have been a swell president, but he didn't know how to pose for his portrait.' Having finished Roosevelt's caricature, which he later gave to Harry Hopkins, Low, by invitation of the president, remained in the Oval Office for one of his press conferences, and noticed how he knew every journalist by first name – he was surprised by how informal and amiable it was throughout. Roosevelt started by saying: 'Well boys, what are we discussing today? Not politics I hope!'

Question: 'How's the campaign going, Mr President?'

Answer: 'Traveling about is costing me a lot for laundry, Fred.'

Question: 'What are the odds, Mr President?'

David Low's caricature of President Roosevelt, drawn in the Oval Office from life.

Answer: 'I've got my bet locked in the safe with the result, Harry.'

It was not the way the then British prime minister Stanley Baldwin would have conducted a press conference, but Low found himself wishing it was. Although it now seems remarkable that Roosevelt granted Low a private sitting, the president had a soft spot for British cartoonists – Low and contemporaries such as Sidney Strube, Leslie Illingworth and Percy 'Poy' Fearon had their work syndicated in many American newspapers at the time. In 1935, FDR had requested the original artwork of a cartoon from the the *Daily Express* by Strube, who had depicted him as the survivor of numerous political scrapes. The president personally wrote to Strube on receipt of the cartoon, stating, 'I am, as Teddy Roosevelt would say, dee-lighted to have that amazingly good cartoon, and I am having it framed for my own study. I hope the next instalment will show that I am still not sunk.'

Low and Vicky visited the United States during the 1948 presidential election campaign. Both cartoonists travelled around the country with the incumbent President Truman. Low even travelled on the president's campaign train, while Vicky attended a press conference given by Truman and made a sketch of him that the president then signed. Vicky shook hands with the president and thanked him. When Truman asked what for, Vicky responded: 'For looking more like my caricature of you then I ever thought you would!' *Daily Mail* cartoonist Leslie Illingworth told a similar story after meeting Lyndon Johnson at the White House in June 1968. 'He's an agreeable man,' said Illingworth – 'fitted my cartoons exactly.' It was David Low who became the first British cartoonist to attend a party convention, the 1948 Republican event in Philadelphia that he attended for *Life* magazine. To Low, it was a wonderful spectacle, especially when compared to British party conferences: 'The Republicans provided a better show than could be found in England anywhere except at the Derby. I half expect to see the winner brought in with a blue ribbon about his neck.' To Low, it seemed more like a sporting spectacular than a political event: 'A British stranger to American politics might have been excused for mistaking in the milling parades, the singing, badges, cardboard elephants, waving portraits and slogans, the comic hats and the unstoppable band a confusion suggestive of a Boat Race night and Derby Day held together in the Albert Hall . . .'

Much more recently, Steve Bell was also dazzled by the scale and the spectacle of an American party convention – apart

David Low covered the 1948 Republican convention for *Life* magazine.

from Gonzo artist Ralph Steadman, he is the only current British cartoonist to have been to one. Bell described his experience at the 2004 Democratic convention in Boston as like a British party conference to the power of ten. According to Bell: 'The razzmatazz is unbelievable, the crowds are vast, the noise is tremendous, the grins are huge and it's a sea of faces. The thing that struck me most was all the signs with different slogans saying things like "May God bless America". There were so many stars and stripes flags! If you saw that many flags in Britain you would think you were at a fascist rally, but both Republicans and Democrats are crazy for the old red, white and blue. It's dazzling – completely unlike anything in the UK.'

During the convention, Bell sat through many speeches by leading Democrats, and Barack Obama, the then little-known senator from Illinois, caught his eye. 'I saw Obama and I didn't know him from Adam, but he gave a terrific speech and had everyone in the convention hall entranced.' In 2008, Bell was again in America, this time for the Republican Convention in Denver, where he saw Sarah Palin give her speech as the presumptive vice-presidential nominee: 'At the time, I didn't have a clue who Sarah Palin was. Believe it or not, she gave quite an impressive display because this

was a big, big hall and she had it in the palm of her hand; I mean it was evil crap but she was giving them what they wanted. In comparison, John McCain, the presidential nominee, was a useless speaker – a poor little guy with funny arms, he looked like a chipmunk. The poor, red-blooded Republicans wanted something in the hall to cheer about, so Palin came on and everyone went crazy. It was fun, and great to observe it.' Unlike David Low and Steve Bell, Ralph Steadman did not enjoy the convention experience. He covered the 1972 Republican and Democratic conventions with Hunter S. Thompson, and scathingly referred to the events as 'smug self-congratulating festivals of establishment assholes.'

Ralph Steadman covered the 1972 Republican convention for *Rolling Stone*.

The experience also left him with a visceral hatred of Richard Nixon – he loved to draw the president, but loathed him personally and politically, and even now compares him to 'a poor man's Donald Trump'.

Perhaps the most remarkable story about British cartoonists and presidential elections is that of Vicky, who covered the 1960 Democratic convention for the *Evening Standard*. On the flight to the convention in Los Angeles, he sat next to Senator John F. Kennedy, sharing his company for six hours. Writing about the flight on the day Kennedy was elected president, Vicky said: 'I had the unique opportunity to talk to the new president of the United States, to study him and do several sketches.' Kennedy actually signed one of the sketches for Vicky, telling him, 'You've made me look rather old.' Vicky noted that, although Kennedy had all the physical attributes and self-confidence to appeal to the electorate, his eyes seemed to give something away. According to Vicky: 'This handsome young American face with the charming Lindbergh-ian, toothy smile is dominated by strange, cold unsmiling eyes that seem too old. It was this expression I concentrated on and he spotted it. I have rarely met a more self-assured young man. When I asked him what he thought of his chances, he replied quietly: "Oh, it's all tied up."'

Vicky sat next to the future President Kennedy on a flight to the Democratic convention in Los Angeles in 1960.

As I discussed in last year's edition of this anthology, British cartoonists tend to be on the left of the political divide, and so they are generally more sympathetic to Democrat nominees than Republicans. This can prove problematic, as Peter Schrank explains: 'As the choices can be so polarizing, there's a danger of going too easy on one candidate. For example, Barack Obama practically reached sainthood status while running for office, which made it very hard to come up with anything that wasn't bland, and even fawning.' This time around, there was no chance of that happening with either candidate, especially in the case of Donald J. Trump. According to Morten Morland: 'The problem with the most recent two campaigns [2008 and 2012] was that, while they were historically significant, they weren't particularly interesting, beyond Obama. This time around there has been an element of peril, which fired things up no end. A campaign featuring Clinton and Trump has been extremely good for cartoonists, I think, explosive in content, but also one that British newspapers have followed more closely than usual, giving cartoonists more opportunity to join in.' Some cartoonists I have spoken to are underwhelmed by both candidates at the time of writing, but the majority fear a Trump victory. The choice, according to Andy Davey is between 'A big fat, gilded, be-quiffed turd riding an elephant, versus your dull auntie from Arkansas on a donkey carrying too much baggage. Risk versus safety, on steroids.'

Donald Trump is a gift for cartoonists. According to Brian Adcock: 'Drawing cartoons about Trump is like shooting fish in a barrel. There's so much to aim at – the hair, the fake tan, the arrogance, the delusion, the vanity, the list goes on and on. Obviously the hair, for me and I think many other satirists, is the main focus of attention. He is hiding his baldness with a wispy comb-over! It reflects his vanity, delusion and arrogance. He is basically saying, "Look at me, I have a full head of hair and so I am virile and strong and should be allowed to govern you." I find myself screaming at the TV, "It's a comb-over, Donald! You're a bald twat!"' Dave Brown has drawn Trump's hair as a separate entity from the rest of him – first as a lemming, showing how his Republican supporters are following him off a metaphorical cliff. Later, he drew Trump's hair as a ferret, symbolising his aggression towards his rivals for the nomination, and later 'Crooked' Hillary. Steve Bell, influenced by New York comic artist Eli Valley's phallic depiction of Trump's hair, morphed his hair into a 'cock and ball' weave; Valley had created this 'tag of identity' after Trump, in an exchange with Marco Rubio during a television debate, boasted that he had a large penis, and Bell decided to do the same. Morten Morland has long had difficulty drawing Trump's hair: 'Annoyingly for me, I still struggle to get his most prominent feature right. I have the same issue with Boris [Johnson].'

In Steve Bell's depiction of Donald Trump and his phallic hairstyle, Bell, at the request of the *Guardian*, changed the word 'penis' to 'manhood'.

Christian Adams, who always draws Trump with the same shouty expression, is also perplexed by his hair. Adams even asked his colleague Matt, cartoonist at the *Telegraph*, how Trump's hair works. A perplexed Matt replied: 'No one knows . . .'

A number of cartoonists feel Trump is actually beyond satire. This, Morten Morland believes, has made things tricky: 'You almost can't ridicule him any more than he unwittingly manages to ridicule himself.' On the other hand, he has the policies and personality of a crazed dictator, which makes trying to undermine him all the more enjoyable. Brian Adcock, like many cartoonists, is perturbed by the thought of President Trump: 'How is it possible that this lunatic is here, in this position? It's unbelievable, it's extraordinary and it's utterly terrifying.' But Bob Moran is not worried. In fact he would be delighted if Trump became president because he thinks it would make his job easier.

'Donald Trump has joined the likes of Boris Johnson and Nigel Farage in the box labelled "gifts that keep on giving". He is also significant for cartoonists by being instantly recognisable; few people in Britain could identify a caricature of Ted Cruz or Bernie Sanders, but they know you have drawn Trump from nothing more than a hairstyle. It seems to me that Donald Trump represents so much of what we in Britain find worthy of satire about American culture: excessive wealth, deluded self-importance, bizarre cosmetic taste and the ability to talk for extended periods without actually saying anything at all. Professionally, I'd be rather pleased if he ended up as the next president.' On a more cautious note, Peter Brookes believes that cartoonists should be careful what they wish for, as 'although Trump would be great to draw, it would be terrible for the world if he was elected.'

The 2016 Democratic candidate presents a very different challenge to cartoonists. Women are often more difficult to caricature because they generally have softer, smoother features. Cartoonists struggled with Mrs Thatcher when she first came to prominence and instead tended to focus more on her hats and handbag, only in her later years developing a distinctive likeness. Clinton is 14 years older than Thatcher was when she came to power, and age has made her easier to caricature. Christian Adams says: 'Her buck teeth are a good feature, although it's a shame they are not that pronounced, but her hamster cheeks are a wonderful asset for me.' Morten Morland believes that there are rich pickings to be had because of 'Hilary's history and baggage and, of course, there is Bill'. However, some cartoonists find Clinton rather uninspiring, or even slightly dull. According to Bob Moran: 'Aside from the fact that she is a woman, there is nothing I find particularly interesting about Hillary Clinton.' That said, the nominees in 2016, and Trump in particular, have offered cartoonists an avalanche of opportunities compared to their rather uninspired vice-presidential picks, and Mike Pence and Tim Kaine have hardly featured in cartoons during the campaign. Asked for his view on them, Martin Rowson said: 'I don't know who

either of them are, and I'm really not paying much attention to this presidential election – we've got more than enough mad shit right here at home . . .'

In 2015, I wrote about how some cartoonists had got into trouble covering British elections in the past. I could only find one anecdote regarding American elections that caused trouble, and for religious rather than political reasons. During the 2004 presidential election, Andy Davey at *The Times* drew John Kerry as 'a many armed Indian deity, since he was presenting himself as the godlike veteran of Vietnam and trying to be all things to all men, spreading himself thinly in policy areas. One of his arms carried a gun (depicting defence policy, as I recall) but an irate reader complained that I had demeaned Hindu deities by giving him a gun. I hadn't intended to depict any particular god, so I don't know which one he thought I was depicting, but there are Hindu deities carrying weapons (not guns, but lethal weapons, nevertheless). I have no idea why cartoonists are expected to reply to crank readers. Do the papers really value these mad people? Perhaps in future cartoonists will be asked to reply to all online comments below the cartoon.'

The presidential race between Hilary Clinton and Donald Trump proved an incredibly fertile

Andy Davey's cartoon in *The Times* during the 2004 Presidential elections caused consternation for religious rather than political reasons.

ground for cartoonists. Indeed, many of the best cartoons from the campaign are featured in this book. And for the next four years, at least, the Americans have President Trump/Clinton as their commander-in-chief. Despite him/her becoming the most powerful man/woman in the world, we should not be too down about it. Whatever happens and however grim things may become, at least we in Britain can continue to laugh daily at the president, thanks to the best cartoonists in the world.

THE CARTOONS

2 September 2015
Brian Adcock
Independent

UKIP leader Nigel Farage blamed the European Union for the increase in migrants, after net migration to the UK reached record levels, according to the Office for National Statistics. According to the cartoonist: 'Nigel Farage is a joy to draw. I mean, just look at his face. Getting the point across with no words is always satisfying.'

David Cameron claimed the government was doing all it could to prevent illegal immigration. Although the country was accepting its fair share of asylum seekers, Cameron said, he wanted to stop people from getting in 'without permission'. This statement came just after over forty migrants had died on an overcrowded boat in the Mediterranean. According to the cartoonist: 'The photograph of little Alan Kurdi lying dead on a Turkish beach had a profound impact. When choosing the subject for that particular week I couldn't ignore it, but to quote it directly seemed inappropriate and exploitative.'

6 September 2015
Peter Schrank
Independent on Sunday

7 September 2015
Morten Morland
The Times

At a meeting of the Parliamentary Labour Party, Tom Watson announced that plans by Jeremy Corbyn supporters to force every Labour MP to face reselection would lead to disunity and act as a 'destructive and destabilising force'. Yvette Cooper urged the government to show more responsibility for the thousands of refugees crossing into Eastern Europe, Greece and Italy, saying Britain had to be true to its values and history by helping the people fleeing turmoil in the Middle East.

According to the cartoonist: 'David Cameron authorised the use of drones in Syria to kill two British subjects accused of planning domestic terrorist acts – the first time killer drones have been used by the government in a country the United Kingdom was not at war with.'

12 September 2015
Ingram Pinn
Financial Times

Jeremy Corbyn was elected Labour leader in a stunning victory that dwarfed even the mandate given to Tony Blair in 1994. He won with nearly 59.5% of first-preference votes, beating rivals Andy Burnham (19%), Yvette Cooper (17%) and Liz Kendall (4.5%). According to the cartoonist: 'I drew this cartoon on the day that Corbyn was elected leader so that it could go straight into the following day's *Observer*. Originally I had drawn Andy Burnham's head sticking out of Corbyn's part of the panto horse, but with a tight deadline looming we couldn't be sure he was on board, so I had to cover him up with white paint. As it turned out, he accepted the post of shadow home secretary in Corbyn's cabinet.'

13 September 2015
Dave Simonds
Observer

MOUNT LOSEMORE...

Italian prime minister Matteo Renzi said that the election of Jeremy Corbyn proved that Labour 'delighted in losing'. 'I think Cameron is the happiest of all about Corbyn's win,' said Renzi, adding, 'It's not a question of being Blairite or anti-Blairite, it's a matter of "Do you want to go to elections like you go to the Olympics, to win or to participate?"... I don't think people who want to get out of NATO want to win elections.' Corbyn's elevation to Labour leader and his 'scruffy' appearance brought back memories of Michael Foot, who was vilified for appearing to wear a donkey jacket at the Cenotaph on Remembrance Sunday in 1981.

14 September 2015
Peter Brookes
The Times

BRIGHTON ROCK...

Left-wing union leaders were delighted by the election of Jeremy Corbyn as Labour leader, which they saw as a sign that public opinion was shifting in favour of direct action against the government. Arriving in Brighton for the TUC annual conference, Mark Serwotka, head of the civil service union the PCS, said: 'You'll see lots of smiling faces at this conference, unlike normally when we come and people look a bit miserable.' Corbyn was given a hero's welcome when he addressed the TUC conference and was enthusiastically applauded when he stated that the government had 'declared war' on workers.

16 September 2015
Dave Brown
Independent

Jeremy Corbyn was criticised for not singing the national anthem at a commemoration service for the 75th anniversary of the Battle of Britain. He was seen standing alongside Defence Secretary Michael Fallon, as *God Save the Queen* was played. Former military commanders, as well as Labour and Tory MPs, said Corbyn had been 'dishonourable' for refusing to sing. The Labour leader later insisted that he had 'stood in respectful silence' during the remembrance ceremony.

16 September 2015
Steve Bell
Guardian

20 September 2015
Chris Riddell
Observer

Apart from criticism for not singing the national anthem, Corbyn was faced with divisions in his new shadow cabinet after Lord Falconer warned that he would step down if Corbyn campaigned to leave the European Union. In a further blow to Corbyn's leadership, it emerged that up to 100 Labour MPs were preparing to defy Corbyn by preparing to publicly campaign for Britain to stay in the EU 'with or without' the new leader's support.

According to the cartoonist: 'Tim Farron took over as leader of the Liberal Democrats from Nick Clegg, who resigned after the party's decimation in the general election. Farron claimed that, with Labour veering more to the left and the Tories to the right, the Lib Dems could claim the centre ground. However, with only eight MPs left after the election (down from 57), I depicted the Lib Dems' centre ground as a desolate island of irrelevance in the middle of nowhere.'

21 September 2015
Ben Jennings
Guardian

German chancellor Angela Merkel stated there would be no legal limit to the number of asylum seekers Germany would be prepared to take in. Merkel was speaking as thousands of exhausted refugees were transported from Hungary into Austria, with most thought to be en route to Germany. Merkel stated that 'the right to political asylum has no limits on the number of asylum seekers . . . As a strong, economically healthy country we have the strength to do what is necessary and ensure every asylum seeker gets a fair hearing.'

21 September 2015
Steve Bright
Sun

BITTEN ...

David Cameron publicly denied the allegation made in a biography co-written by the former Tory donor Lord Ashcroft that he had participated in a bizarre university club ritual involving a dead pig's head. *Call Me Dave* made other allegations about Cameron's Oxford University lifestyle, including stories about him smoking cannabis with friends and hosting a party at which cocaine was available.

22 September 2015
Dave Brown
Independent

Chancellor of the Exchequer George Osborne embarked on a week-long visit to China to boost commercial and political ties with the country. The Treasury said that he wanted to 'foster a new era in UK-China relations'. Speaking ahead of his trip, Osborne said the delegation was about 'exploring new opportunities to open up new markets'. The trip came ahead of a state visit to the UK by Chinese president Xi Jinping the following month, the first by a Chinese leader for ten years.

26 September 2015
Martin Rowson
Guardian

Jeremy Corbyn suffered a major blow to his authority when a bid by the Labour leadership to press for a vote on the renewal of the Trident nuclear programme was overwhelmingly rejected at the Labour party conference in Brighton. According to the cartoonist: 'Punch and Judy is a great trope to use in a cartoon, and with the Labour conference by the sea in Brighton and with Jeremy Corbyn at odds with some of his comrades, it all fitted together rather neatly.'

28 September 2015
Brian Adcock
Independent

30 September 2015
Ian Knox
Irish News

Jeremy Corbyn pledged to deliver 'a kinder politics and a more caring society' as he used his first conference speech as leader to urge the Labour party to unite behind him to oppose 'the misery on offer from the Conservatives'. Lord Mandelson, Tony Blair and Gordon Brown had all warned of the dangers of a Corbyn leadership prior to his election as leader, while Cameron and Osborne claimed Corbyn was a threat to both Britain's national security and her economic revival.

Jeremy Corbyn was criticised by senior Labour colleagues for saying he would not fire Britain's nuclear weapons if he were prime minister. Corbyn said nuclear weapons 'didn't do the USA much good on 9/11' and added that he was elected leader on a platform opposing Trident renewal. Shadow Defence Secretary Maria Eagle said his words were 'not helpful', while Shadow Foreign Secretary Hilary Benn said Corbyn should abide by the party's decision on renewing Trident. David Cameron said Corbyn's comments showed Labour could not be trusted with Britain's national security.

1 October 2015
Christian Adams
Daily Telegraph

According to the cartoonist: 'As someone who loves the cinema, I always enjoy using images from films – although this one, based on the closing shot of Stanley Kubrick's *Dr. Strangelove*, is so famous that many people don't know where it came from. Kubrick is one of the film-makers that cartoonists quote most: the axe through the door in *The Shining*, the murder in the underpass and Malcolm McDowell's look in *A Clockwork Orange*, the apes and the mysterious black monolith in *2001 . . .*'

4 October 2015
Peter Schrank
Independent on Sunday

In an anti-austerity demonstration organised by the TUC and the People's Assembly, thousands of protesters marched past the Conservative party conference venue in Manchester. A variety of slogans featured on mass-produced and homemade placards, including 'Cut War Not Welfare', 'Don't Bomb Syria', 'No Cuts' and 'Divine Discontent, Divine Disobedience'.

5 October 2015
Martin Rowson
Guardian

6 October 2015
Peter Brookes
The Times

In his speech to the Tory party conference, and billed as an early marker for a leadership bid, George Osborne declared: 'We are the builders.' Osborne set out his plans for a new National Infrastructure Commission, to be led by former Labour minister Lord Adonis.

David Cameron addressed the Conservative party conference for the first time since his party's general election victory in May. The conference was dominated by speculation over his successor as leader. However, Cameron made clear that he intended to remain in charge until the 2020 election. Of his potential successors, Cameron called George Osborne 'the Iron Chancellor' and lavished praise on Boris Johnson as mayor of 'the greatest city on earth', but only gave a passing mention to Theresa May.

7 October 2015
Christian Adams
Daily Telegraph

Jeremy Corbyn was accused of snubbing the Queen as he avoided a ceremony to join the Privy Council. The Labour leader had been expected to attend the swearing-in ceremony, which involved kneeling in front of the monarch and kissing her hand while swearing an oath of allegiance. His aides said he had other commitments including 'some relaxation time' which meant he could not attend.

9 October 2015
Dave Brown
Independent

Deputy Labour leader Tom Watson faced calls to apologise over 'unfounded accusations' against the former home secretary Leon Brittan, after police dropped a rape inquiry against him. Although Watson said he was sorry for the distress caused to the Brittan family, he insisted he had had a 'duty' to inform police of sex abuse allegations against Lord Brittan, who died in January 2015, aged 75. Sir Samuel Brittan said Tom Watson 'should apologise to my sister-in-law [Lady Brittan] for making unfounded accusations against my brother'.

10 October 2015
Peter Brookes
The Times

According to the cartoonist: 'Vladimir Putin stepped up Russian military aid to President Assad's besieged army in Syria and I drew a cartoon criticising his intervention. What surprised me after it was published was the heated critical response I received in the comment section of the paper asking why I hadn't drawn a cartoon depicting the Western powers' handling of the Syrian crisis. The West's response to events in Syria has been shambolic, but on that weekend I drew the cartoon it was Russian bombers pounding Syria and it's damned difficult going after all the "evil doers" in one drawing.'

11 October 2015
Dave Simonds
Observer

... AND WITH A SINGLE BOUND HE WAS FREE !

Labour backbenchers reacted furiously after the shadow chancellor John McDonnell did a U-turn on a pledge to vote for George Osborne's 'fiscal charter', which committed the government to running a surplus in 'normal times'. In his defence, McDonnell stated: 'Originally what I said to people was, "Look, this charter is a political stunt, a political trap by George Osborne. It is virtually meaningless. He never meets his targets. This is just a stunt. Let's ridicule it in the debate and vote for it because it is a meaningless vote." '

14 October 2015
Dave Brown
Independent

14 October 2015
Steve Bell
Guardian

The British government bowed to intense pressure and pulled out of a controversial £5.9 million prison services deal with Saudi Arabia amid concerns over human rights. Downing Street stressed that pulling out of the deal was unconnected to the case of expat Karl Andree, jailed in Saudi Arabia after being caught with homemade wine. Despite withdrawing from the prison deal, Justice Secretary Michael Gove insisted Britain would maintain its relationship with the country.

Jeremy Corbyn suffered his first Commons rebellion of his leadership, as 21 Labour MPs refused to vote against the government's new economic rules. Most Labour MPs had not voted for him as leader and some had not held back in their criticism of him. At PMQs, Corbyn repeated his tactic of asking questions submitted by the public. Regarding his attire, Antonia Kraskowski, fashion editor at the *Daily Express*, said: 'In a jacket that looks at least two sizes too big, Jeremy Corbyn looked like he's been playing dress-up in the bargain bin from his local charity shop.'

15 October 2015
Dave Brown
Independent

18 October 2015
Chris Riddell
Observer

Boris Johnson claimed the price of quitting the European Union was 'lower than it's ever been.' Speaking in Japan on a trade visit, he refused to rule out spearheading the Leave campaign. After being invited to join children in Tokyo for a game of non-contact touch rugby, Boris knocked over a ten-year-old child while attempting to score a try. Over dinner at Chequers, David Cameron and Angela Merkel discussed the renegotiation of Britain's EU membership. Cameron told her he wanted to keep Britain in the European Union, but that there was 'much to be worked through' to reach an acceptable deal.

Chinese president Xi Jinping arrived in the UK at the start of a four-day state visit. The first day of President Xi's visit ended with a state banquet at Buckingham Palace with the Queen and Prince Philip. While on an official visit to China in 1986, Prince Philip had told a group of British exchange students staying in the city of Xian: 'If you stay here much longer you'll all be slitty-eyed.'

20 October 2015
Stan McMurtry
Daily Mail

President Xi ended his UK trip at Manchester Airport announcing plans for direct flights between Manchester and Beijing. David Cameron claimed that the government's Northern Powerhouse project was gathering strength and now had 'Chinese backing', while British and Chinese officials said it was the start of a 'golden era' of relations which the Treasury hoped would make China Britain's second biggest trade partner within a decade. The cartoon, when originally published in the *Guardian*, was cropped so that the image of the bare-bottomed Queen was left out for matters of taste.

23 October 2015
Steve Bell
Guardian

The House of Lords forced George Osborne into an embarrassing climb-down when it voted in favour of a Labour motion calling for his proposed cuts to tax credits, which would have cost three million families an average of £1,300 a year, to be delayed for three years. The chancellor pledged to 'lessen' the impact of his changes by introducing 'transitional help' for the poorer families affected. However, he nonetheless vowed to press on with his £12 billion welfare bill reduction.

28 October 2015
Steve Bell
Guardian

30 October 2015
Dave Brown
Independent

David Cameron said he was 'disappointed' after Sir John Chilcot wrote to inform him he would not be ready to publish the much-delayed Iraq Inquiry report until June or July. 2016. The prime minister urged Chilcot to speed up publication of his report, which had already taken seven years to complete and cost the taxpayer £10.3m.

Nigel Farage said it would be 'good news' if Boris Johnson and Theresa May agreed to front the fight for Britain to leave the European Union. Farage was responding to a poll which suggested that the public thought May would be the best choice to lead the official Leave campaign; May did not respond directly when asked whether she would consider such a role, but refused to rule out backing a British exit.

2 November 2015
Steve Bright
Sun

6 November 2015
Steve Bell
Guardian

President George H. W. Bush finally broke his public silence about some of the key figures in his son's administration, issuing scathing critiques of Vice President Dick Cheney and Defence Secretary Donald Rumsfeld. Bush referred to Cheney as 'iron-ass' in asserting too much 'hard-line' influence within George W. Bush's White House. Rumsfeld, Bush Senior said, was an 'arrogant fellow' who could not see how others thought and 'served the president badly'.

David Cameron said it would take 'some time' before British tourists were flown back from the Egyptian resort of Sharm el-Sheikh. The government had grounded all flights in the wake of growing evidence that a Russian Airbus, which crashed after leaving the resort, had been brought down by a terrorist bomb.

8 November 2015
Scott Clissold
Sunday Express

12 November 2015
Steve Bell
Guardian

Jeremy Corbyn, a lifelong republican, took part in a Buckingham Palace ceremony to become a member of the Privy Council. He did not kneel before the Queen as he was sworn in. A Labour spokesman said Corbyn had complied with the usual processes, which usually involved kneeling on a stool before kissing the Queen's hand. Speaking to *ITV News* before the ceremony, Corbyn signalled he would not be kneeling. 'I don't expect to be kneeling at all, no,' he said. 'I expect to be nominated to the Privy Council and that's it.'

David Cameron insisted that a US air strike against an ISIS executioner known as 'Jihadi John' was an act of self-defence. An American official described the attack as a 'clean hit' with no harm to others on the ground. He also said that Mohammed Emwazi, a British subject, was 'eviscerated' upon leaving a building in Raqqa, Syria. Cameron said: '[Emwazi] posed an ongoing and serious threat . . . This was an act of self-defence. It was the right thing to do . . . Britain and our allies will not rest until we have defeated this evil terrorist death cult and the poisonous ideology on which it feeds.'

14 November 2015
Martin Rowson
Guardian

14 November 2015
Bob Moran
Daily Telegraph

A unilateral decision by Germany's interior minister to reverse the country's asylum policy forced Chancellor Angela Merkel to rethink her open-door welcome to Syrian refugees. Critics said her accommodating message had encouraged migrants to pour into Germany in ever-larger numbers, overwhelming the resources of local authorities.

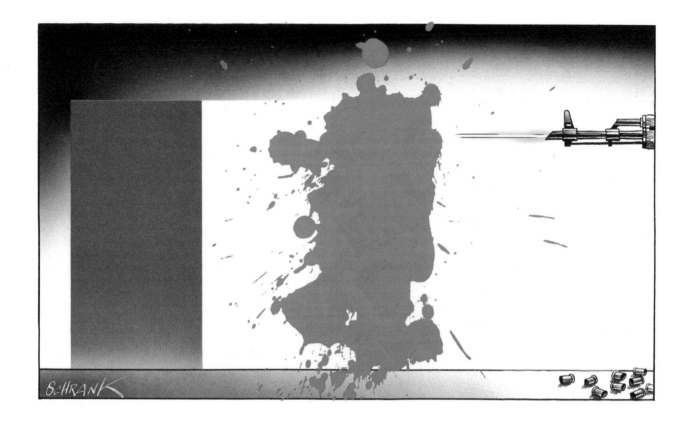

According to the cartoonist: 'This one was tricky. I used to work on my cartoon for the *Independent on Sunday* during the second half of Friday, often finishing quite late. On this particular Friday I was relaxing with a glass of wine, when the 10pm news came on with reports of the attacks in Paris. I knew immediately that I'd have to start again. By the following morning I had two ideas ready. This was actually my fourth attempt, which was conceived in rather a panic. It's a very strong image – I always like using the French flag and the three colours, which stand for *Liberté, Egalité, Fraternité*. So it's *Fraternité* that gets it.'

15 November 2015
Peter Schrank
Independent on Sunday

ALL BEHIND YOU, FRANÇOIS

World leaders expressed compassion and solidarity after the attacks in Brussels that killed 32 people and injured many more, when blasts went off at Brussels Zaventem Airport and on the city's subway. French president François Hollande called the events an attack on all of Europe, and President Obama urged international unity in the fight against terror: 'We will do whatever is necessary to support our friend and ally Belgium in bringing to justice those who are responsible.' The cartoon is based on David Low's famous cartoon of May 1940, 'All Behind You, Winston', which featured Winston Churchill leading his coalition government.

15 November 2015
Bob Moran
Daily Telegraph

SHOULDER TO SHOULDER

Russia suspended all flights to Egypt following confirmation that the plane crash in Egypt's Sinai desert, which killed all 224 Russian holidaymakers on board, was caused by a terrorist bomb. Vladimir Putin vowed to find and punish those responsible and ordered an increase in air strikes on Syria as 'retribution' for the attack.

17 November 2015
Christian Adams
Daily Telegraph

This cartoon provoked hundreds of complaints for appearing to compare Muslim refugees to rats, while Labour MP Richard Burgon claimed it was Islamophobic. Press standards regulator Ipso received 200 complaints regarding the drawing, prompting speculation that *Mail* editors might face investigation. However, the *Mail*'s managing editor's office refused to 'dignify these absurd comments, which wilfully misrepresent this cartoon, with a response. As should be blindingly obvious, Mac's cartoon is a comment on the terrorist atrocities in Paris. The rats were intended to depict terrorists smuggling themselves into Europe amongst innocent refugees.'

17 November 2015
Stan McMurtry
Daily Mail

SECURITY POLICY...

Jeremy Corbyn said he would not be happy with UK police or security services operating a 'shoot-to-kill' policy in the event of a terrorist attack. The Labour leader said that such action could prove 'counter-productive'. He also declined to answer what he called the 'hypothetical question' of whether he would ever back military intervention against extremists. 'I'm not saying I would or I wouldn't,' Corbyn said, stressing the need for a political resolution to be found in Syria. He repeated his criticism of previous interventions in the Middle East, saying they had 'unleashed forces' and boosted extremists.

18 November 2015
Christian Adams
Daily Telegraph

According to the cartoonist: 'This was on the complicated situation in Syria, with so many different nations becoming involved in the war militarily, all with varying agendas and commitments. On this particular day, Turkey shot a Russian plane out of the sky for coming into its airspace, whilst David Cameron was pushing to try and get Britain further involved in the mess.'

25 November 2015
Ben Jennings
Independent

"EVERYTHING UNDER HEAVEN IS IN UTTER CHAOS; THE SITUATION IS EXCELLENT"

CHAIRMAN MAO

Chairman Mao's *Little Red Book* made a surprise appearance in the House of Commons when Shadow Chancellor John McDonnell brandished a copy while accusing the government of relying on Chinese investment. McDonnell started quoting from the book and then threw the copy at Chancellor George Osborne, in an attempt to make a joke about Osborne's decision to sell off some of Britain's public assets to the Chinese.

26 November 2015
Christian Adams
Daily Telegraph

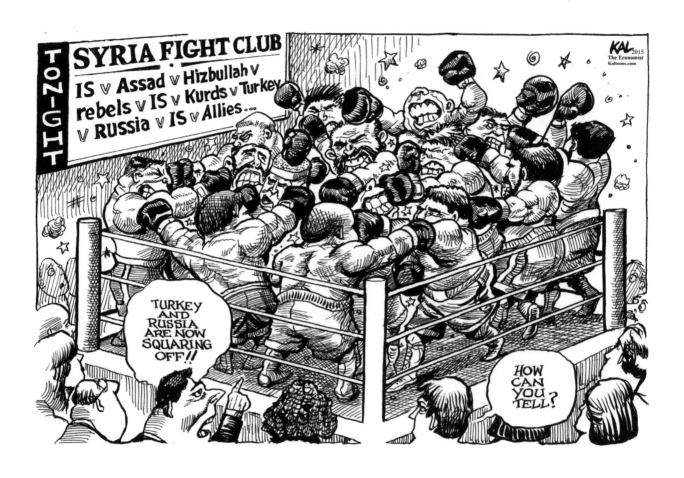

26 November 2015
Kevin Kallaugher
The Economist

Turkish jets shot down a Russian bomber along the Syrian border which, as a result, threatened to undermine attempts to create a new international coalition to confront the expanding ISIS. President Putin accused Turkey of a 'stab in the back' and of aiding terrorists, as Russian state media began conducting a propaganda campaign against Turkey.

David Cameron urged MPs to back British air strikes against ISIS in Syria. Cameron said the UK could not afford to stand aside and argued that it was morally unacceptable to leave the US, France and other allies to carry the burden: 'The longer ISIS is allowed to grow in Syria, the greater the threat it will pose. It is wrong for the United Kingdom to subcontract its security to other countries, and to expect the aircrews of other nations to carry the burdens and the risks of striking ISIS in Syria to stop terrorism here in Britain.'

27 November 2015
Peter Brookes
The Times

It was thought that Jeremy Corbyn wanted to whip Labour MPs into voting against the government's proposed air strikes in Syria, despite strong opposition from within his shadow cabinet. Corbyn sparked anger amongst the Labour front bench after writing to Labour MPs to say he could not back David Cameron's plan for Britain to take part in action on ISIS targets in Syria. Union leader Len McCluskey claimed that Corbyn's opponents were using the row as part of an attempt to oust him and warned that they were 'playing with fire'.

30 November 2015
Morten Morland
The Times

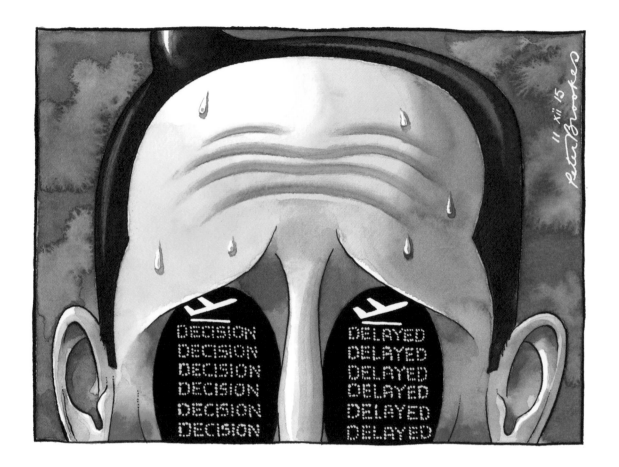

David Cameron was accused of political game-playing by delaying a final decision on whether to press ahead with the expansion of Heathrow Airport. Faced with the possible resignation of Zac Goldsmith MP, who opposed Heathrow's expansion, Cameron deferred a final irreversible decision until after May's mayoral elections. Goldsmith had said he would resign his Richmond Park and North Kingston seat in south-west London if the government backed the plans. The Labour mayoral candidate Sadiq Khan also opposed the expansion, so a delay suited both main parties.

2 December 2015
Peter Brookes
The Times

THE INTERNATIONAL BRIGADE ...

4 December 2015
Dave Brown
Independent

Jeremy Corbyn sat stony-faced as his Shadow Foreign Secretary Hilary Benn sent the Commons into rapturous applause as he made a compelling case for air strikes against ISIS in Syria. Corbyn said: 'I did not agree with it. I was appalled that MPs should clap, shout and cheer when we were deciding to go and bomb somewhere. Parliament is supposed to be serious. It's not a place for jingoistic cheering.' The cartoon is based on 'The Falling Soldier', a famous photograph taken during the Spanish Civil War by Robert Capa.

MPs passed a government motion, by 397 votes to 223, to join US-led coalition air strikes against ISIS militants in Syria. According to the cartoonist: 'After the British parliament's decision to join military air strikes in Syria, I wanted to try and make a simple image of the "collateral damage" that would inevitably occur from adding more bombs.'

5 December 2015
Ben Jennings
i

7 December 2015
Brian Adcock
Independent

Jeremy Corbyn finalised his front bench team by filling posts left vacant after Kevan Jones, Jonathan Reynolds and Stephen Doughty quit in protest at the sacking of shadow cabinet members who had been at odds with the Labour leader. According to the cartoonist: 'This was fun, trying to get to grips with some of those new faces in the Labour Party, a fantastically interesting-looking bunch! For some reason I have drawn Jeremy Corbyn with just one tooth sticking out. I must have been experimenting.'

According to the cartoonist: 'This was after the San Bernardino mass shooting, an all-too-common occurrence in America. This particular shooting was being related to terrorism, but of course the real issue is America's relationship with guns, which a large (and armed!) portion of the country refuses to believe. Here we have a patriotic, fully loaded Uncle Sam thwarting Barack Obama, who is powerless to pursue meaningful laws restricting the American people's easy access to firearms.'

7 December 2015
Ben Jennings
Guardian

10 December 2015
Steve Bell
Guardian

Writing in the *Spectator*, Tony Blair said that anyone who wanted a Labour government recognised 'the tragedy of the Labour party's current position'. In his first comments on the party under the leadership of Jeremy Corbyn, the former prime minister said the party was 'in danger of not asking the right questions, never mind failing to get the right answers'. Blair said the party he used to lead should aspire to govern and not be a 'fringe protest movement'. Blair had been an early critic of Corbyn, warning before his leadership election victory that the party risked 'annihilation' if he won.

UNHINGED

Donald Trump read a statement about preventing Muslims from entering the US after a Muslim husband and wife killed 14 people in San Bernardino, California. Stating that 'we have no choice', he went on to say that the authorities should be looking at 'anger' within mosques, and called on his supporters to report 'violations' without fear of being accused of racial profiling. According to the cartoonist: 'Presidential candidate Donald Trump provoked attacks from fellow Republicans trying to distance themselves from his insane proposal to bar all Muslims from entry to the United States.'

12 December 2015
Ingram Pinn
Financial Times

13 December 2015
Peter Schrank
Independent on Sunday

David Cameron said he did not expect an agreement to be reached on his EU reform aims at December's summit of European leaders. The prime minister said 'good progress' had been made, but that the scale of the UK's aims meant he would not get an agreement 'in one go'. Cameron spoke to Angela Merkel about the renegotiation efforts, and told her a deal would not be possible at this stage. According to the cartoonist: 'I love drawing boats, but avoid drawing crowds of people whenever possible. The trade-off between the two resulted in one of my own favourite drawings of the last year or two.'

GIVING TURKEY A GOOD STUFFING...

18 XII 15 Peter Brookes

Vladimir Putin subjected Turkey to a furious tirade, accusing her of shooting down a Russian warplane to curry favour with the United States. Addressing almost 1,400 reporters, the Russian president asserted that he saw no prospect of a rapprochement with Ankara. Putin had imposed economic sanctions on Turkey and made it clear that they would stay in place for some time, accusing the current Turkish leadership of 'creeping Islamisation' that would have the secular state's founder, Kemal Ataturk, turning in his grave.

18 December 2015
Peter Brookes
The Times

18 December 2015
Christian Adams
Daily Telegraph

David Cameron signalled that the EU referendum would take place in 2016 as he prompted fury from Eurosceptic backbenchers by making it clear he intended to campaign for Britain to Remain. The prime minister said that staying in a reformed European Union was 'vital' for Britain's economic and national security. This started rumours that cabinet ministers were poised to resign in protest. The film *Star Wars Episode VII: The Force Awakens* was released in the UK on 17 December.

THE SPECIAL ONE LOSES THE DRESSING ROOM...

MY WHOLE TEAM IS REVOLTING!

CARSWELL 1

UKIP MP Douglas Carswell called on Nigel Farage to step down as leader, to help the party draw a line under its unpleasant and socially illiberal image. Carswell had frequently clashed with Farage in the 18 months since his defection from the Conservatives, but this was the first time he had called for him to resign outright. Although he praised Farage's achievement in growing the party, he said sometimes a start-up 'needs to change gear and to change its management if it's to go the next level'. Chelsea had just sacked its manager José Mourinho because of a 'palpable discord with the players' according to the club's technical director, Michael Emenalo.

19 December 2015
Peter Brookes
The Times

24 December 2015
Morten Morland
The Times

Chancellor George Osborne received little festive cheer when it emerged that Britain's economy had grown less than previously thought. Data from the Office for National Statistics revealed that growth had only been 0.4% in the three months to the end of September, down from the initial estimate of 0.5%.

According to the cartoonist: 'There were a couple of cases of British citizens not being allowed to enter America (one family were on their way to Disneyland), which many put down to unfair discrimination based on them being Muslims. This was not long after Donald Trump had also made a promise to ban any Muslims from entering America if he became president. As the cartoon was published on Boxing Day, I gave the story a Yuletide theme, with Santa Claus stopped by US border control due to a "suspicious beard".'

26 December 2015
Ben Jennings
Guardian

WITHOUT A PADDLE...

28 December 2015
Christian Adams
Daily Telegraph

Angry Labour party supporters demanded to know why Jeremy Corbyn had not travelled to York to meet with those flooded out of their homes, as criticism of his handling of the crisis mounted. The floods, which had plagued large areas of northern England, were met with an unusual wall of silence from the Labour leader, despite much of the worst devastation taking place in Labour heartlands.

David Cameron was accused of abusing the honours system after Lynton Crosby, who oversaw the Tories' general election campaign, was awarded a knighthood in the New Year's honours list. Labour MP Paul Flynn, who sat on the Public Administration and Constitutional Affairs Committee, said it would 'drive the honours system into deeper disrepute', whilst Shadow Home Secretary Andy Burnham called the decision to honour Crosby 'outrageous'.

1 January 2016
Morten Morland
The Times

David Cameron said he wanted to stamp out what he called 'spurious' legal claims against British troops returning from war. Cameron had asked ministers to draw up plans to curb claims, including restricting 'no win, no fee' arrangements. Lawyers responded to the prime minister by saying that no one was above the law, and that many abuse cases had been proven. About 280 former UK military personnel were still being investigated by the Iraq Historic Allegations Team for allegations of murder, abuse and torture of Iraqi civilians. Defence Secretary Michael Fallon criticised what he called 'ambulance-chasing British law firms' and argued that there was 'a strong case' for suspending the European human-rights law when sending forces into action overseas.

5 January 2016
Stan McMurtry
Daily Mail

SHOCK WAVES

According to the cartoonist: 'North Korean president Kim Jong-Un claimed to have tested a hydrogen bomb. South Korea responded by playing loud propaganda music across the border.'

9 January 2016
Ingram Pinn
Financial Times

9 January 2016
Martin Rowson
Guardian

Three Labour MPs resigned from the party's front bench in protest at sackings made by Jeremy Corbyn in his reshuffle. Tough new guidelines issued on alcohol cut recommended drinking limits and stated that there was no such thing as a safe level of drinking. The UK's chief medical officers said new research showed any amount of alcohol can increase the risk of cancer. The new advice says men and women who drink regularly should consume no more than 14 units a week, equivalent to six pints of beer or seven glasses of wine.

Tim Peake carried out the first ever spacewalk by an 'official' British astronaut, when he and another astronaut replaced a faulty component on the international space station's exterior. Peake tweeted condolences to the family of David Bowie, who had died aged 69, following an 18-month battle with cancer.

10 January 2016
Scott Clissold
Sunday Express

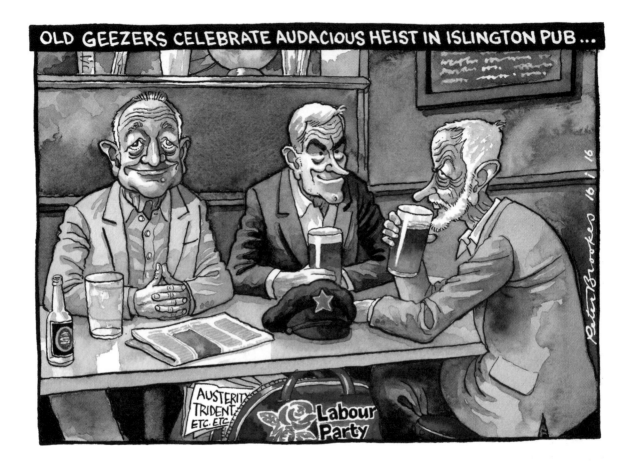

OLD GEEZERS CELEBRATE AUDACIOUS HEIST IN ISLINGTON PUB...

Ken Livingstone dismissed allegations from a recently sacked Labour frontbencher that he was running the Labour leadership with a 'bunch of far-left anti-war communists' in tow. The former London mayor laughed off claims from the former shadow culture secretary Michael Dugher that he was pulling the strings of Labour's high command from behind the scenes. Jeremy Corbyn had removed Dugher from his post for 'disloyalty' and 'incompetence'. A gang in the £14m Hatton Garden jewellery raid were facing jail after the final three were convicted.

10 January 2016
Peter Brookes
The Times

Health Secretary Jeremy Hunt vowed to continue his drive for 'high-quality care, seven days a week' in the NHS after junior doctors announced they would go on strike. The action came after the British Medical Association and the government failed to reach an agreement on a proposed new contract for junior doctors. The BMA, which was concerned about pay for weekend working, career progression and safeguards to protect doctors from being overworked, said the strike had sent a 'clear message' to the government. However, Jeremy Hunt described the walkout as 'completely unnecessary' and urged junior doctors to return to the negotiating table.

13 January 2016
Steve Bell
Guardian

Alleged victims of sexual abuse by Greville Janner hit out at the decision to drop court proceedings against the late peer, saying it amounted to 'an establishment cover-up'. A long-awaited independent report into why it took decades to bring Lord Janner to court to face child sex abuse charges was due to be published. The CPS and Leicestershire Police were expected to face severe criticisms from retired judge Richard Henriques for mishandling investigations into the late peer. One solicitor who represented Janner's alleged victims said the report could shed light upon claims that the police were pressured by politicians to drop their previous inquiries. One alleged victim said that the decision to drop proceedings would increase suspicion of 'an establishment cover-up from day one' that stopped Janner from appearing before the courts.

16 January 2016
Martin Rowson
Guardian

David Cameron announced plans to encourage greater integration of Muslim women in Britain. The prime minister said that Muslim women who had come to the UK on spousal visas without learning the language could be denied leave to remain. He said there would be no guarantee that those who did not improve their English could stay, claiming there were 38,000 Muslim women who could not speak English and 190,000 with limited skills in the language.

19 January 2016
Christian Adams
Daily Telegraph

BUNCH OF CREEPS...

23 January 2016
Peter Brookes
The Times

David Cameron and George Osborne defended the deal the government had made with Google over tax. Google had agreed to pay £130 million in tax dating back to 2005 to HMRC, which said it was the 'full tax due in law'. European MPs however, described it as a 'very bad deal' and Labour said it amounted to a 3% tax rate. Former Business Secretary Vince Cable said Google had 'got off very, very lightly' and the chancellor had 'made a fool of himself' by hailing the deal as a victory. In 2013, Google had paid around £20 million in taxes in the UK. In the same year it achieved UK sales of £3.93 billion.

David Cameron said that Russia's actions in relation to the murder of Alexander Litvinenko in 2006 were 'absolutely appalling'. The prime minister said a public inquiry showed the murder had been 'state-sponsored'. The inquiry believed Putin had likely signed off the poisoning of Litvinenko with polonium-210 in part due to personal 'antagonism' between the pair. Home Secretary Theresa May said the murder was a 'blatant and unacceptable' breach of international law.

24 January 2016
Chris Riddell
Observer

24 January 2016
Bob Moran
Daily Telegraph

Jeremy Corbyn was given a tour of the Grande-Synthe migrant camp in northern France and met migrants and aid workers. The Labour leader said conditions in the camp near Dunkirk would be a 'disgrace anywhere', and Britain should be 'part of bringing European support to people'. He said the long-term solution was to deal with the conflicts causing the migration crisis: 'What I'm trying to achieve here is to understand the nature of the refugee crisis that's facing the whole of Europe.'

STORM TRUMP...

Donald Trump stormed ahead in the polls during the Iowa primaries, topping the 40% mark for the first time. That more than doubled the support of his nearest competitor, Ted Cruz (19%), with no other candidate in double-digits. The Republican establishment now had to consider the once-unthinkable idea of a Trump nomination. A huge blizzard had begun to dump snow on the eastern United States, stalling the momentum of the Iowa campaign, as candidates made their final push across the state.

25 January 2016
Morten Morland
The Times

GIVE ME YOUR TIRED, YOUR POOR,
YOUR HUDDLED MASSES YEARNING TO BREATHE FREE,
THE WRETCHED REFUSE OF YOUR TEEMING SHORE,
SEND THESE THE TEMPEST-TOST TO ME ...
I'LL LIFT THEIR WALLETS, JEWELS,
GOLD TEETH AND MORE !

27 January 2016
Dave Brown
Independent

The Danish Parliament backed a controversial proposal to confiscate asylum seekers' valuables to pay for their upkeep. Police would be allowed to seize valuables worth more than 10,000 kroner (£1,000) from refugees, to cover housing and food costs. A spokesman for UN Secretary General Ban Ki-moon criticised the decision, saying refugees deserved compassion: 'People who have suffered tremendously, who have escaped war and conflict, who've literally walked hundreds of kilometres if not more and put their lives at risk by crossing the Mediterranean should be treated with compassion and respect, and within their full rights as refugees.'

DANCE LIKE A BUTTERFLY, STING LIKE A BUNCH OF MIGRANTS

During a Commons clash over the refugee crisis with Jeremy Corbyn, David Cameron was condemned for describing people in a camp in Calais as a 'bunch of migrants'. The Refugee Council said Cameron's comments were 'disappointing' and called on him to show leadership in response to the situation.

28 January 2016
Steve Bell
Guardian

A new book revealed that Jeremy Corbyn had 'showed off' a naked Diane Abbott to impress his friends when he was a young Labour activist. The Labour leader invited fellow activists to his London flat where they were 'shaken' to find Abbott in his bed. In a 1985 interview Abbott described her 'finest half-hour' as being when she romped with a naked man in a Cotswold field. She described Corbyn as a 'long-time friend and very close' ally. Meanwhile, a primary school head teacher in Darlington had written to parents asking them to stop dropping their children off in their pyjamas.

31 January 2016
Bob Moran
Daily Telegraph

'All right, Mr Assange. You can stay a bit longer, but as you're now officially dead, Lord Lucan – you can hop it!'

A UN legal panel ruled that WikiLeaks founder Julian Assange should be allowed to walk free and be compensated for his 'deprivation of liberty'. Assange, who faced extradition to Sweden over a rape claim, sought asylum in London's Ecuadorean embassy in 2012. Assange said it was a 'really significant victory that has brought a smile to my face'. However, the Foreign Office said the report 'changes nothing' and it would 'formally contest the working group's opinion'. A High Court judge ruled that Lord Lucan was now presumed to be dead, 42 years after vanishing when his children's nanny Sandra Rivett was bludgeoned to death in London. Lucan was declared dead in 1999, despite dozens of unverified sightings, but the new ruling gave his son the right to inherit the family title.

5 February 2016
Stan McMurtry
Daily Mail

FIRST HURDLE

6 February 2016
Ingram Pinn
Financial Times

According to the cartoonist: 'The race for US presidential candidates started in Iowa with Ted Cruz beating Donald Trump to win the Republican vote, and for the Democrats, Bernie Sanders holding Hillary Clinton to a virtual tie.'

Boris Johnson launched a fierce attack on David Cameron's EU renegotiation, claiming the prime minister had failed to deliver: 'I wanted to persuade myself that reform would happen. There's been no real change . . . Unless we make a stand now we will simply wake up on June 24 with absolutely nothing changed.' According to the cartoonist: 'The poster for the first *Jaws* film has become a classic of its genre, often quoted by cartoonists. Equally the line "You're gonna need a bigger boat" from the same film has entered the bloodstream of our language. I was pleased to combine them both in the same image.'

7 February 2016
Peter Schrank
Independent on Sunday

Dozens of Tory party members accused David Cameron of disrespecting the party's grassroots after he had told MPs to disregard their views on Europe. In a letter to the *Daily Telegraph*, the signatories from more than 40 Conservative associations had said their opinions should be heard. They said it was 'deeply regrettable' that the PM had dismissed their views. Downing Street told the newspaper that the prime minister had the 'greatest of respect for Conservative associations. He was simply making the point that everyone should ultimately vote with their conscience.'

7 February 2016
Bob Moran
Daily Telegraph

Jeremy Hunt insisted that a new contract would be imposed on junior doctors, as he rejected suggestions that he did not have the power to force through the changes. The health secretary had faced questions from his Labour counterpart, who had suggested that Hunt might have misled Parliament and needlessly provoked unprecedented strike action from medics. Hunt hit back, accusing Labour of staging 'a truly desperate' attempt at a diversion from the question of whether they will back the doctors' strikes. Junior doctors promised to fight on after the government announced it would impose a new contract on the profession. The stance raised the prospect of more strikes, while behind the scenes there was talk of legal action, mass resignations and doctors refusing to sign contracts.

14 February 2016
Chris Riddell
Observer

15 February 2016
Brian Adcock
Independent

According to the cartoonist: 'When Donald Trump blurted his way onto the political scene, I imagined every cartoonist in the world did a high five with the nearest person to them. He is a walking cartoon and provides you with tons of material to work with – it's like shooting fish in a barrel. This cartoon followed one of his debates where his performance reminded me of a sulky child, and the cartoon was born.'

David Cameron began a crucial week in his renegotiation of Britain's membership of the EU. The prime minister embarked on final discussions in Brussels, where he hoped to secure a new deal for the UK that the majority of his party would support. Downing Street said cabinet ministers could not speak out until the cabinet has met to agree a government position. The PM had reportedly bowed to pressure from anti-EU ministers including Iain Duncan Smith not to delay calling the cabinet meeting – it was claimed that this would give the Remain campaign an unfair head start.

16 February 2016
Christian Adams
Daily Telegraph

'I assure you, William is not backing the EU. All members of the royal household are completely unbiased.'

Kensington Palace denied that Prince William publicly suggested Britain would be better off staying in Europe. The Duke of Cambridge used a speech at the Foreign Office to emphasise the importance of our 'ability to unite in common action with other nations'. Standing next to Foreign Secretary Philip Hammond, he said: 'Right now, the big questions with which you wrestle – in the UN, NATO, the Middle East and elsewhere – are predicated on your commitment to working in partnership with others.' The timing of his comments drew comparisons to the Queen's intervention on the eve of the Scottish referendum, when she urged Scots to 'think very carefully about the future'. However, a Kensington Palace spokesman insisted that Prince William's speech was not about Europe. 'He does not mention the word Europe once.'

18 February 2016
Stan McMurtry
Daily Mail

"EVER CLOSER UNION....?"

David Cameron said that a deal he had struck with the EU would give the UK 'special status' and that he would campaign with his 'heart and soul' to stay in the union. Cameron claimed that the new agreement would allow the UK power to limit some EU migrants' benefits, and that the UK would no longer be bound to 'ever-closer union' with other EU member states. Brexit campaigners in the Tory party claimed the 'hollow' deal offered only 'very minor changes'. According to the cartoonist: 'When I was at secondary school I did a mural on a wall for an art project and it looked a lot like this. It had about 200 school kids in it, and they were all fighting and acting in a ridiculous manner, just like our glorious leaders.'

22 February 2016
Brian Adcock
Independent

"WITH DEAFENING ÉCLAT..."

22 February 2016
Morten Morland
The Times

After days of speculation, Boris Johnson announced he would back the campaign for the UK to leave the European Union. Johnson said the decision came with a 'huge amount of heartache', and the last thing he wanted was to go against the government. The previous week he had told the BBC's *Sunday Politics*: 'I'm going to wait until the prime minister does his deal, and I will then come off the fence with deafening *éclat*.'

As Republican primaries opened on Super Tuesday in 12 US states, Donald Trump appeared well placed to sweep them all, save Texas, where Ted Cruz was set to win on home turf. The dawning reality of Trump, who at the start of the campaign had been viewed by many as something of a joke, as the party favourite left senior Republicans scrambling to either destroy or join his populist bandwagon.

24 February 2016
Kevin Kallaugher
The Economist

26 February 2016
Steve Bell
Guardian

Deputy Labour leader Tom Watson revealed that he had told David Cameron personally that he would back the Tory government in any Commons vote to renew the weapons system, with the construction of four new 'Successor' submarines. Watson said it was important to give 'certainty' to defence manufacturers, allies and enemies that Britain would keep its nuclear deterrent despite Jeremy Corbyn's trenchant opposition.

'Amazing isn't it? I wasn't aware of this either.'

The BBC missed opportunities to stop 'monstrous' abuse by Jimmy Savile and Stuart Hall because of a 'culture of fear', a report said. The Dame Janet Smith review said BBC culture 'was deeply deferential' and staff were reluctant to speak to managers about complaints. Director General Lord Hall said that the BBC had failed to protect the victims. The review found that senior managers were not told of complaints about Savile because of an 'atmosphere of fear', and a small number of BBC managers in Manchester had been aware of Hall's activities. Dame Janet said Savile and Hall had been 'serial sexual predators' and the BBC had missed five clear opportunities to stop their misconduct.

27 February 2016
Stan McMurtry
Daily Mail

Iain Duncan Smith accused David Cameron of having 'a low opinion of the British people' by downplaying the UK's prospects if it left the EU. This came after Cameron accused Tory MPs backing an EU exit of wanting to take 'the gamble of the century' with the country's future. Amid rising tensions, some Tory ministers and backbenchers had threatened a no-confidence vote in the prime minister unless he scaled back his criticisms of Boris Johnson and other Eurosceptics. One senior backbencher said that if hostilities did not cease they would have 'no problem' getting the 50 MPs' signatures required to force such a vote, while another leading Eurosceptic was reported to have said: 'He's trying to pick a fight with us. It will bite him in the a***.'

29 February 2016
Morten Morland
The Times

Sanctioned!

In a move aimed specifically at Iain Duncan Smith, Sir Jeremy Heywood, the cabinet secretary, issued new guidelines to ban civil servants from preparing new research for anti-EU cabinet ministers that could be used in the EU referendum campaign. Downing Street had feared that Duncan Smith, who had strong doubts about the welfare elements of the prime minister's EU reform plan, would seek to ask his officials to assess the credibility of the plan. Heywood faced allegations that he was acting in a constitutionally improper manner.

29 February 2016
Martin Rowson
Guardian

Former Conservative chancellor Norman Lamont came out in favour of an EU exit, calling the upcoming referendum a 'once-in-a-generation opportunity'. The Conservative party was deeply split over the referendum, with about half of its MPs supporting an EU exit against the PM's recommendation. Five cabinet members, including Work and Pension Secretary Iain Duncan Smith, backed the Vote Leave campaign. The government published an analysis of the UK's options if it left the EU, suggesting they would all be worse for the economy than staying in. Foreign Secretary Philip Hammond said the aim was to 'smoke out' Leave campaigners who had 'avoided' spelling out their vision of a post-EU Britain, while Leave campaigners said the 'dodgy dossier' was misleading.

3 March 2016
Christian Adams
Daily Telegraph

Fairy Tale Wedding of the Cent~~ury~~ ENARIAN

Rupert Murdoch and Jerry Hall marked their marriage with a service of celebration at St Bride's Church near Fleet Street in London. It is the 84-year-old Murdoch's fourth marriage and the first for Miss Hall, 59, after her 1992 Bali wedding to Sir Mick Jagger was later deemed legally void. Rebekah Brooks, chief executive of News UK, and her husband Charlie were at the service.

5 March 2016
Martin Rowson
Guardian

GOP DEBATE...

5 March 2016
Morten Morland
The Times

The Republican presidential race got dirty as Donald Trump opened the GOP debate by boasting about the size of his genitals. He responded to comments from Marco Rubio in which the Florida senator had joked about the size of Trump's hands and said, 'You know what they say about men with small hands.' On the debate stage, Trump stretched his hands out for the audience to see, and then insisted the suggestion that 'something else must be small' was false. 'I guarantee you there's no problem,' Trump said, to howls from the audience.

The EU pressed Turkey, through which many migrants pass, to take back some refugees, in return for $3.3bn in aid. Turkey's President Erdoğan accused the EU of failing to deliver on the promised aid. Turkey, he said, was sheltering more than 2.7 million refugees from the civil war in neighbouring Syria, while the EU wanted Turkey to do more to patrol its own waters. German chancellor Angela Merkel said she anticipated a 'difficult discussion', as a rift emerged among EU powers on the closure of the main route through the Balkans.

8 March 2016
Dave Brown
Independent

11 March 2016
Stan McMurtry
Daily Mail

Five men were jailed for the £14 million Hatton Garden safety deposit box jewellery raid in April 2015: three ringleaders each received seven years, while two other men were given six and seven years respectively. The mastermind, Brian Reader, was too ill to attend after suffering a second stroke and would be sentenced later. Sentencing them, the judge said: 'The burglary at the heart of this case stands in a class of its own.'

SPECIAL RELATIONSHIP...

According to the cartoonist: 'This cartoon was on US-UK relations after Obama gave a lengthy interview to *The Atlantic*, in which he appeared to criticise David Cameron for being "distracted" during military action in Libya. This raised questions of whether the "special relationship" was under strain, so I had the idea of Obama and Cameron both sat on the Oval Office's sofa, with a clear distance between them. Within this we see a Blair and Bush-shaped groove in the furniture, where their predecessors had enjoyed cosier ties. Part of what inspired this one was a memory of Homer Simpson's well-formed groove in his sofa.'

12 March 2016
Ben Jennings
Guardian

13 March 2016
Peter Schrank
Independent on Sunday

Approximately five years had passed since the popular protest against Bashar al-Assad's regime began in Syria, a movement that spiralled into a blood-drenched civil war and claimed the lives of nearly half a million people. After years of battle, murder and massacre, no end to the conflict appeared to be in sight. According to the cartoonist: 'This was my second to last cartoon for the *Independent on Sunday*, before it went online only and my slot was axed. I always enjoy drawing strong and gloomy images, not necessarily looking for a laugh, but for an image with emotional impact.'

It was claimed that Chancellor George Osborne's cuts to disability benefits could cause 200,000 disabled people to each lose almost £3,000 a year. The decision to cut Personal Independence Payments (PIP) made to over 640,000 people, in a bid to save the Treasury £1.2 billion, would remove 200,000 disabled people from the system. In addition, 400,000 further people would experience a reduction in their weekly payments.

15 March 2016
Dave Brown
Independent

22 March 2016
Steve Bell
Guardian

David Cameron heaped praise on Iain Duncan Smith in the House of Commons after the latter had resigned from the cabinet over plans to cut benefits for the disabled. Cameron then confirmed in Parliament that he was ditching the controversial planned cuts that George Osborne had announced in the budget.

On 22 March, three coordinated terrorist attacks occurred in Brussels. Two nail bombs exploded at the city's airport, and one at a metro station. In these attacks, 32 victims and three terrorists were killed, and over 300 people were injured. Another bomb was found during a search of the airport. ISIS claimed responsibility for the attacks; the bombings were the deadliest act of terrorism in Belgian history, and the country's government declared three days of national mourning.

23 March 2016
Morten Morland
The Times

Nigel Farage insisted he had been 'wholly justified' to link the Brussels attacks and EU migration rules. David Cameron said he did not think it 'appropriate' to use the Brussels attacks to further arguments in the EU referendum debate. But the UKIP leader said those campaigning for the UK to stay in the EU had already 'politicised' the security issue after the Paris attacks. Boris Johnson had been accused of exaggerating and misrepresenting the case for Brexit by the Conservative chairman of the Commons Treasury Committee.

24 March 2016
Dave Brown
Independent

David Cameron was handed a gift at PMQs after *The Times* had revealed an internal Labour party list which ranked its MPs on how loyal they were to Jeremy Corbyn from 'core' to 'hostile'. In a nod to the bitter Tory in-fighting over the abandoned cuts to disability benefits and the EU referendum, the prime minister said, 'I thought I had problems.'

24 March 2016
Steve Bell
Guardian

27 March 2016
Chris Riddell
Observer

There had been growing signs of discontent among backbenchers on both sides of the House of Commons with their respective leaders. The film *Batman v Superman: Dawn of Justice* was released in British cinemas on 25 March.

Russian president Vladimir Putin congratulated Syrian president Bashar al-Assad on retaking the ancient city of Palmyra from Islamic State terrorists. Putin stressed the importance of preserving the UNESCO World Heritage Site – the Russian air force had made 40 flights over the area of the Syrian city of Palmyra in the previous 24 hours, hitting 117 targets and killing over 80 militants.

28 March 2016
Martin Rowson
Guardian

29 March 2016
Ben Jennings
Guardian

According to the cartoonist: 'Shortly after the tragic terrorist attack in Brussels earlier this year, Donald Trump warned Americans to not travel to Europe, saying it was too dangerous. I thought it was especially ironic that a man who encourages violence to his gun-toting flock and has made certain statements that have been considered tantamount to a war crime, was saying *Europe* was too dangerous.'

'All is not lost. It seems there really is such a thing as reincarnation.'

Britain rejected Argentine claims to the waters surrounding the Falkland Islands following a UN commission ruling that extended the South American nation's maritime territory by 35%. Downing Street dismissed the move as 'not legally binding', and insisted that the UN commission did not have jurisdiction over national sovereignty. According to the UN, Argentine waters had expanded 1.7 million square kilometres to encompass the disputed Falklands, or, as they are known in Argentina, Islas Malvinas.

30 March 2016
Stan McMurtry
Daily Mail

Boris Johnson said he 'passionately' agreed with Nigel Farage that hospital staff should be able to speak English, after the UKIP leader had called for doctors and nurses who could not speak the language properly to be 'winnowed out' of the NHS. A British man who posed smiling for a photo with a hijacker on board an EgyptAir flight has said he did it to take 'a closer look' at the apparent explosives belt, adding: 'I figured if his bomb was real I'd nothing to lose anyway.' He was one of three passengers and four crew held hostage after Seif Eldin Mustafa hijacked the EgyptAir flight bound for Cairo from Alexandria and forced it to be redirected to Cyprus.

31 March 2016
Peter Brookes
The Times

MADE IN CHINA

STEEL

I AM UPPER CLASS, BUT I LOOK UP TO HIM BECAUSE HE IS MORE POWERFUL ...

... I LOOK DOWN ON HIM BECAUSE HE IS A WORKER ...THOUGH NOT MUCH LONGER !

David Cameron claimed the government was 'doing everything it could' to save thousands of steel jobs, but warned there was 'no guarantee of success'. The prime minister also said nationalisation was 'not the right answer' after Tata Steel's decision to sell its UK business. However, the government was accused of opposing EU moves to impose higher tariffs on Chinese steel entering Europe. The cartoon is also a tribute to Ronnie Corbett who had died on 31 March, aged 85. It is based on a classic *Frost Report* sketch about Britain's class system which juxtaposed the diminutive Corbett with the taller Ronnie Barker and the towering John Cleese to represent the working, middle and upper classes.

1 April 2016
Dave Brown
Independent

A BIGGER SPLASH

2 April 2016
Ingram Pinn
Financial Times

According to the cartoonist: 'South Africa's Constitutional Court ruled that President Jacob Zuma defied the constitution in refusing to repay the state for lavish improvements to his private home, including a swimming pool and amphitheatre.'

Barack Obama used his final nuclear security summit to deliver the stark warning that 'madmen' could kill and injure hundreds of thousands of innocent people using plutonium the size of an apple. According to the cartoonist: 'I was staring at the nuclear symbol wondering what I could do with it, as there was this story about President Obama being concerned that ISIS might get their hands on some nuclear material. I then thought, "Ooh, I wonder if it could pass as a butterfly?"'

3 April 2016
Brian Adcock
Independent

David Cameron's spokesperson said his father's links with offshore accounts revealed in a huge leak were a 'private matter'. The late Ian Cameron, who died in 2010, was among hundreds of individuals named in the cache of documents dubbed the Panama Papers. Cameron's father used a Panama-based legal firm to shield an investment fund called Blairmore Holdings Inc. Asked whether the prime minister's family still held money in offshore arrangements, his spokesperson replied: 'That is a private matter, I am focused on what the government is doing.'

5 April 2016
Steve Bell
Guardian

Donald Trump's crushing loss to Ted Cruz in Wisconsin netted the Republican front runner just six delegates. He forewent his typical election-night speech after losing the state by 13% and his campaign instead fired off a blistering statement suggesting he had been cheated and slamming the Texas senator for being in on the con.

6 April 2016
Christian Adams
Daily Telegraph

David Cameron defended a government pro-EU membership campaign, amid criticism that £9 million of public money was being spent on 'one-sided propaganda'. The PM said the government was 'not neutral' in the referendum and the cost was 'money well spent'. Nigel Farage said it was 'outrageous' to spend taxpayers' money 'to tell us how we should think and how we should vote' and Leave campaigners complained that the promotional campaign was costing more than the £7 million each side was allowed to spend by law.

8 April 2016
Peter Brookes
The Times

David Cameron finally admitted he had benefited from a Panama-based offshore trust set up by his late father. After three days of stalling and four statements issued by Downing Street, he confessed that he sold shares in January 2010 for £31,500, a profit of £19,000, just before becoming prime minister in 2010. He said he had sold up before entering Downing Street 'because I didn't want anyone to say I had other agendas or vested interests'.

8 April 2016
Dave Brown
Independent

Jeremy Corbyn warned there could be a 'bonfire' of workers' rights if the UK voted to leave the EU in June. David Cameron said they disagreed on 'lots of things' but welcomed Corbyn's backing for EU membership, though Leave campaigners suggested that the Labour leader 'did not really mean it'. Making his first major speech of the referendum campaign, Mr Corbyn stood by his past criticisms of the EU but said Britain had to remain in to fight for social reform. Meanwhile, a 30-foot model of the Loch Ness monster built in 1969 for a Sherlock Holmes film was found almost 50 years after it sank in the loch.

14 April 2016
Christian Adams
Daily Telegraph

Party leaders both past and present joined forces to attempt to persuade people to back the Remain campaign. David Cameron was flanked by ex-Lib Dem leader Paddy Ashdown and Labour's Neil Kinnock for the telephone campaigning session, ahead of the first official day of the EU campaign. Meanwhile, the gagging order imposed over a 'celebrity threesome' case descended further into farce after a Scottish newspaper published full details of the mystery couple behind the controversial injunction.

16 April 2016
Peter Brookes
The Times

17 April 2016
Brian Adcock
Independent

According to the cartoonist: 'Due to the high level of salt, sugar and fat in its sauces, Dolmio took the unprecedented step of putting warning labels on its bottles. If only our politicians and their shenanigans came with such a warning.'

Labour called for Culture Secretary John Whittingdale to withdraw from involvement in press regulation after news of his relationship with a sex worker. Four newspapers knew about the relationship, which ended in 2014, but decided not to publish the story. Shadow Culture Secretary Maria Eagle said it had left him 'vulnerable' to pressure from the press. Whittingdale, who said that he had not known the woman was a sex worker, said the relationship had not affected his decisions. As culture secretary, part of Whittingdale's job was to regulate newspapers, and he subsequently considered introducing a new regulatory framework into press standards.

17 April 2016
Chris Riddell
Observer

20 April 2016
Christian Adams
Daily Telegraph

After George Osborne said that if Britain left the EU the UK would be 'permanently poorer', Michael Gove hit back by accusing the government of 'treating voters like children who can be frightened into obedience'. Gove also accused those campaigning for Britain to remain of making a 'deeply pessimistic' and 'negative' argument.

President Obama urged the UK to stick with the EU, as he began his final trip to Britain as US president by having lunch with the Queen. Obama stated that being in the EU magnified Britain's influence across the world. He did acknowledge that ultimately the matter was for British voters to decide for themselves, but he also said: 'The outcome of your decision is a matter of deep interest to the United States. The tens of thousands of Americans who rest in Europe's cemeteries are a silent testament to just how intertwined our prosperity and security truly are.' In response, David Cameron tweeted: 'The US is one of our closest allies. So it's important to hear Barack Obama on why we should remain in the EU.'

23 April 2016
Bob Moran
Daily Telegraph

Brush up your Shakespeare

"What bloody man is that?"
Macbeth, Act I, scene 2

"It is a tale
Told by an idiot, full of sound and fury
Signifying nothing."
Macbeth, Act V, scene 5

"Cry God for Bozza, Bozza
and Saint Boz!!!"
Much Aboz About Boris.
All of it.

"Now cracks a noble heart. Good-night, sweet prince; And flights of angels sing thee to thy rest."
Hamlet, Act V, sc. 2

23 April 2016
Martin Rowson
Guardian

Boris Johnson criticised President Obama after he advised Britain to stay in the EU and suggested his attitude to Britain was based on his 'part-Kenyan' heritage and 'ancestral dislike of the British empire'. Writing a column for the *Sun*, Johnson recounted a story about a bust of Winston Churchill purportedly being removed from the White House. 'Some said it was a snub to Britain. Some said it was a symbol of the part-Kenyan President's ancestral dislike of the British Empire – of which Churchill had been such a fervent defender,' he wrote.

Home Secretary Theresa May made her first major speech of the referendum campaign – she asserted that Britain would flourish outside the EU, but urged voters to vote Remain to help protect the country from the threat of terrorism. However, she listed a host of reasons why it was 'nonsense' to suggest that the UK was too small to cope outside the EU, in contrast to David Cameron and George Osborne, who refused to accept that leaving could have any positive consequences.

24 April 2016
Steve Bell
Guardian

In a scathing attack, a government source claimed the two junior doctors' strikes that week were aimed at toppling the government and Health Secretary Jeremy Hunt. The British Medical Association said the accusation was 'ridiculous'. It came as medical leaders called on the prime minister to end the stand-off, warning it posed a 'significant threat to our whole health system'. Thirteen senior organisations, including the leaders of ten royal colleges, wrote to David Cameron to say it was his responsibility to intervene to bring both sides back to the negotiating table.

26 April 2016
Peter Brookes
The Times

Former London Mayor Ken Livingstone was suspended from the Labour party, after saying Hitler had supported Zionism in the 1930s 'before he went mad and ended up killing six million Jews'. He made the comments while defending Labour MP Naz Shah over accusations she was anti-Semitic. According to Livingstone: 'If you look at what this is all about, it's not about anti-Semitism in the Labour party . . . What this is all about is actually the struggle of the embittered old Blairite MPs to try to get rid of Jeremy Corbyn.'

30 April 2016
Morten Morland
The Times

1 May 2016
Chris Riddell
Observer

The Times said it had made a 'mistake' in not having the Hillsborough verdicts on the front page of its first edition. The newspaper said it had fixed the error before its second edition. *The Times* was criticised along with the *Sun*, which also left news of the inquest verdicts off its front page. The *Sun* had published an article entitled 'The Truth' days after the tragedy in 1989, alleging that fans were to blame, but the inquest's jury exonerated Liverpool supporters. Rupert Murdoch, owner of the *Sun*, came out and backed Brexit.

The Tory London mayoral candidate, Zac Goldsmith, accused Labour candidate Sadiq Khan of being friendly with terrorists: 'The number one job of any Mayor of London is to keep our city safe. Yet if Labour wins, we will have handed control of the Metropolitan Police, and with it control over national counter-terrorism policy, to a party whose candidate and current leadership have, whether intentionally or not, repeatedly legitimised those with extremist views.' Kahn accused Goldsmith of being 'desperate and divisive'. Andrew Boff, the former leader of the London Assembly's Conservative group, said that he and many other Tories in the capital were 'really troubled' by the Goldsmith tactic of painting Labour's candidate as an extremist.

2 May 2016
Morten Morland
The Times

2 May 2016
Christian Adams
Daily Telegraph

Jeremy Corbyn came under renewed pressure as new details emerged about Labour's failure to tackle anti-Semitism within the party. A dossier compiled by the *Telegraph* included a series of disturbing examples of anti-Semitic attitudes among party activists and leading members. It followed the suspension from the party of Ken Livingstone and Naz Shah for making anti-Semitic comments. Labour had announced an independent inquiry, but Livingstone, suspended after saying that Hitler supported Zionism, refused to withdraw his statements and claimed the Israeli prime minister agreed with him.

ON ANOTHER GRASSY KNOLL ...

Donald Trump emerged as the presumptive Republican presidential nominee after a resounding victory in Indiana, as Ted Cruz suspended his presidential campaign. It now looked likely that Trump would face off against Hillary Clinton, a former secretary of state and first lady. She was within sight of clinching the Democratic nomination, a goal that had eluded her in 2008 when she lost out to Barack Obama.

5 May 2016
Dave Brown
Independent

9 May 2016
Christian Adams
Daily Telegraph

Sadiq Khan used his first major interview as Labour's Mayor of London to attack his leader Jeremy Corbyn. In highly pointed remarks, Khan said Labour under Mr Corbyn was simply not doing enough to address the concerns of ordinary voters. He also warned that unless Corbyn changed his tack and reached out to the whole electorate – not just natural Labour supporters – then the party's central mission to improve the lives of ordinary working people would be put in jeopardy.

David Cameron warned that peace in Europe would be at risk if Britain voted to leave the EU. Britain has regretted 'turning its back' on Europe in the past, he said, arguing the EU had 'helped reconcile' countries and maintain peace. In response, Boris Johnson hit back, saying that the EU's 'anti-democratic tendencies' were 'a force for instability and alienation'. During his speech, Boris, encouraged by reporters, gave a brief rendition of *Ode to Joy*, the European Union's official anthem, in German.

10 May 2016
Martin Rowson
Guardian

The Queen was filmed saying that Chinese officials were 'very rude' during the previous year's state visit by President Xi Jinping, while discussing their treatment of Britain's ambassador to China with a senior police officer at a Buckingham Palace garden party. This came after David Cameron was overheard saying that Afghanistan and Nigeria were 'fantastically corrupt'. The police authorities complained to the *Guardian* about the cartoon, stating that it was inappropriate to portray a senior police officer in this way. In the version of the cartoon that appeared online, the policewoman was saying, 'I could murder a Chinese!'

12 May 2016
Steve Bell
Guardian

Culture Secretary John Whittingdale said that the BBC must put 'distinctive content' at its heart. It was part of a major overhaul of the BBC, unveiled by the government. Whittingdale made clear he was 'emphatically not saying the BBC should not be popular'. The culture secretary was referring to earlier speculation that the Corporation would not be allowed to schedule popular programmes such as *Strictly Come Dancing* in prime slots. Responding to Mr Whittingdale's statement, Maria Eagle, the shadow culture secretary, said: 'We know the secretary of state is extremely hostile to the BBC. He wants it diminished in size.'

13 May 2016
Dave Brown
Independent

Sir John Major launched an attack on senior Conservatives supporting Brexit, accusing them of exaggerating arguments to exit the EU. He said that claims by Michael Gove, Boris Johnson and Iain Duncan Smith did not bear scrutiny and he warned about the tone of some exit campaigners' rhetoric on immigration. Mark Carney, governor of the Bank of England, warned that the risks of leaving 'could possibly include a technical recession'. Vote Leave campaigners strongly criticised Carney, with one calling for him to resign. Meanwhile, David Cameron visited Abbey Road Studios to meet with leading figures from the creative industries.

14 May 2016
Morten Morland
The Times

OVERCROWDING

TORY CELLBLOCK - EU

David Cameron hoped to reunite his party after the EU referendum by promising to lead a 'progressive, one-nation government' that would focus on improving young people's life chances. With senior Conservatives attacking each other almost daily, the government used the Queen's Speech to present a full legislative programme, promising to reform schools, prisons and the adoption system. The task facing Cameron in unifying his party after the referendum was underlined by harsh criticism from the Eurosceptic former cabinet minister Iain Duncan Smith, who accused the prime minister of deliberately avoiding controversy in the run-up to the vote. Prison reformers dismissed the government's planned shake-up of prisons as a 'tragic distraction' that would not solve key problems of overcrowding and underfunding.

19 May 2016
Christian Adams
Daily Telegraph

21 May 2016
Peter Brookes
The Times

Jeremy Hunt admitted that the entire health budget had not in fact been protected in George Osborne's spending review. He made the admission to the Health Select Committee, saying there would be shortages in funding, the majority of which would be seen in local health budgets. Figures revealed that the NHS had a £2.45 billion black hole in its budget, with 65% of trusts reporting a deficit as they struggled with flatlining budgets and growing patient demand.

George Osborne warned that Britain would face a year-long 'DIY recession' following a vote to leave the EU. The chancellor was about to present a Treasury analysis into the short-term economic impact of Brexit, which would claim GDP would be 3.6% lower after two years than it would be if Britain voted to remain. It also warned of a sharp rise in inflation, with house price growth hit by 10%, comparing the expected uncertainty to that experienced in the early 1990s recession.

24 May 2016
Morten Morland
The Times

It emerged that Lord Sugar, star of *The Apprentice* and the government's new enterprise tsar, had previously been fiercely critical of George Osborne. Sugar, a former Labour peer who was signed up by David Cameron to launch a campaign to encourage young people to start their own business, said of the chancellor in a 2012 interview: 'I never rated him in the beginning. I don't know what his qualifications are to be chancellor, but we need someone in there who's got a handle on the economy ... I don't know if there'll be a reshuffle, but if I were David Cameron I would seriously think about it.'

26 May 2016
Steve Bell
Guardian

The World Health Organization rejected a call to move or postpone the Rio Olympic Games over the Zika outbreak. It said this would 'not significantly alter' the spread of the virus, which is linked to serious birth defects. In an open letter to the organization, more than 100 leading scientists had said new findings about Zika made it 'unethical' for the Games to go ahead. They also said the global health body should revisit its Zika guidance.

29 May 2016
Brian Adcock
Independent

According to the cartoonist: 'During the EU referendum, the infighting between the Tory party was particularly brutal, and when I came to do this cartoon a story about a child who had crawled into a gorilla enclosure at a zoo in Cincinnati was getting people talking, so I used the old cartooning trick of merging the two stories together. The actual event sadly ended in the zoo shooting and killing the gorilla, yet in this cartoon's scenario, it's Cameron who has wriggled himself into this tricky spot, and is calling out for the same action to be taken against the unpredictable "Borilla", who is hungry for the PM's job, while the spectating members of his party, doubtful of Cameron's leadership, turn the other way.'

31 May 2016
Ben Jennings
Guardian

David Cameron said he was proud to campaign with Sadiq Khan to stay in the EU, weeks after claiming Labour's London mayor was unfit for office because of alleged links to Islamist extremists. The prime minister was accused of participating in a racist campaign against Khan during the mayoral contest, but the two politicians buried the hatchet as Cameron praised Khan for being a 'proud Muslim, a proud Brit and a proud Londoner'. Speaking in Roehampton, south-west London, Cameron said: 'Let me first of all congratulate Sadiq on his victory. He talked about his father. He's the son of a bus driver. I'm the son of a stockbroker, which is not quite so romantic.'

1 June 2016
Steve Bell
Guardian

Jeremy Corbyn dismissed suggestions that he was not getting Labour's Remain message across to voters. This came after a major union leader had accused Corbyn of running a 'lacklustre' and 'half-hearted' campaign to keep Britain inside the EU. The Labour leader said the EU could 'deliver positive change' on issues ranging from mobile phone charges to clean beaches and protecting bees, but at the same time called for reform and pledged to oppose the new EU-US trade deal.

3 June 2016
Peter Brookes
The Times

Tributes poured in from all over the world to boxing legend Muhammad Ali, who died at the age of 74. President Obama said, 'Muhammad Ali shook up the world. And the world is better for it.' The three-time world heavyweight champion, one of the world's greatest sporting figures, had been suffering from Parkinson's disease.

5 June 2016
Scott Clissold
Sunday Express

7 June 2016
Dave Brown
Independent

Hilary Clinton finally clinched the Democratic nomination for US president after reaching 2,383 delegates, the required number to make her the presumptive nominee, and the first female nominee for a major US political party. However, rival Bernie Sanders said Mrs Clinton had not won, as she was dependent on Super Delegates who could not vote until the party convention in July.

Tony Blair and John Major joined forces to warn that Brexit would 'tear apart the UK'. The former prime ministers and political adversaries shared a platform in Northern Ireland to warn that leaving the EU would be a 'historic mistake' and would mean 'throwing all the pieces of the constitutional jigsaw into the air'.

10 June 2016
Dave Brown
Independent

Blower 11.6.16

11 June 2016
Patrick Blower
Daily Telegraph

According to the cartoonist: 'As the Brexit referendum reached its climax, MPs from both sides of the House switched sides. Labour MP John Mann announced he was switching from Remain to Leave while Labour's Khalid Mahmood and Tory MP Sarah Wollaston both defected to Remain.'

According to the cartoonist: 'As the Queen celebrated her second 90th birthday, the EU debate raged on, in which we heard a lot about kowtowing to the unelected leaders in Brussels. I liked the irony of depicting the most patriotic of Leave campaigners deriding these unelected officials whilst being part of the crowd at the monarch's celebrations. One Leave supporter said the cartoon was a sign of Remain "getting desperate". I say that comment was a sign that Brexiteers couldn't take a joke.'

11 June 2016
Ben Jennings
i

Nigel Farage was accused of adopting Nazi-style propaganda tactics to help win the EU referendum. The UKIP leader unveiled a new poster showing a vast queue of refugees stretching into the distance, with the headlines 'Breaking Point' and 'The EU has failed us all' – Michael Gove said he 'shuddered' when he saw it. Farage deployed a fleet of vans emblazoned with the image to follow him around central London – defending his poster amid attacks from all sides of the political spectrum, he claimed that 'all' the people pictured in the photograph would have EU passports within years.

17 June 2016
Steve Bell
Guardian

LOSING GROUND

A CNN poll put Hillary Clinton ahead of Donald Trump by a 47% to 42% margin in the race for the American presidency, with only 22% of registered voters saying that their minds would change before November. Both candidates had been plagued by mediocre ratings, each being viewed unfavourably by nearly six in ten voters, and neither had wrapped up universal support within their own party.

18 June 2016
Ingram Pinn
Financial Times

HATE DOESN'T HAVE
A CREED, RACE OR RELIGION,
IT IS POISONOUS.

BRENDAN
COX

19 June 2016
Chris Riddell
Observer

Labour MP Jo Cox was murdered near Birstall Library in West Yorkshire, just after she had concluded a drop-in session for constituents. Her husband urged people to 'fight against the hatred that killed her', as tributes flooded in. According to Brendan Cox: 'She would have wanted two things above all else to happen now: one, that our precious children are bathed in love, and two, that we all unite to fight against the hatred that killed her. Hate doesn't have a creed, race or religion, it is poisonous.'

A former chair of the Conservative party switched her support from the Leave campaign to that for Remain. Baroness Warsi stated that the 'hate and xenophobia' of the Leave campaign was 'a step too far'. She said she realised she could no longer support Leave when she saw UKIP's 'Breaking Point' poster. Vote Leave said it was not aware Lady Warsi had joined its campaign in the first place, while Nigel Farage defended the poster, calling it 'the truth'.

21 June 2016
Brian Adcock
Independent

23 June 2016
Peter Brookes
The Times

During the BBC's *Great Debate* in Wembley Arena, Boris Johnson got a standing ovation from his supporters after his closing statement, in which he declared: 'Thursday can be our country's independence day.' David Cameron dismissed as 'nonsense' Johnson's rallying call to vote Leave, and insisted Britain would not be 'shackled to a corpse' by voting to remain. Meanwhile, the film *Independence Day: Resurgence* was released in British cinemas on 24 June.

Playtime's over...

The UK voted to leave the EU. Not long after the count was completed, David Cameron appeared in front of 10 Downing Street to announce that he would step down by October, saying the country deserved a leader committed to carrying out the withdrawal. The stunning turn of events was accompanied by a plunge in the financial markets, with the value of the pound and stock prices plummeting; the margin of victory startled even proponents of a British exit, with the Leave campaign winning by 52% to 48%. More than 17.4 million people voted Leave, while about 16.1 million voted to remain.

25 June 2016
Martin Rowson
Guardian

Senior pro-Brexit politicians attempted to distance themselves from some of the promises they had made during the EU referendum campaign. Iain Duncan Smith claimed he had 'never said' the National Health Service would get £350 million a week extra after leaving the EU. Labour MP Yvette Cooper said the conduct of Boris Johnson and Michael Gove had been 'utterly shameful', and accused them of deliberately lying to voters and putting community cohesion at risk after their warnings over mass migration from Turkey.

27 June 2016
Morten Morland
The Times

'Taraaa! Your problems are over!'

Roy Hodgson resigned as England manager after a humiliating defeat by Iceland eliminated them from the European Championships. Meanwhile, a motion of 'no confidence' in Labour leader Jeremy Corbyn was passed by the party's MPs in a 172-40 vote. This followed resignations from the shadow cabinet and calls on Corbyn to quit. Corbyn said the ballot had 'no constitutional legitimacy' and affirmed he would not 'betray' the members who voted for him by resigning. The leader's allies told his critics to trigger a formal leadership contest if they wanted to challenge him.

29 June 2016
Stan McMurtry
Daily Mail

AN EXISTENTIAL CRISIS

30 June 2016
Steve Bell
Guardian

Despite having himself resigned, David Cameron used PMQs to heap further pressure on Jeremy Corbyn. Cameron demanded that he step down after the vast majority of Labour party MPs passed a motion of no confidence in their embattled leader. 'It might be in my party's interest for him to sit there,' Cameron told the Commons, 'but it's not in the national interest. And I would say: "For heaven's sake man, go!"' Tom Watson claimed the leadership crisis had put the Labour party in peril – he said the party was facing an 'existential crisis' with Corbyn as leader, and was failing the country.

According to the cartoonist: 'Boris as prime minister was a daunting prospect, so it was both a relief and a shock when Michael Gove betrayed him. The *Independent* editors were understandably not keen on knives in cartoons so soon after the tragic murder of Jo Cox – the usual "stabbing in the back" images were off limits. The famous photo of Boris on the zip wire during the London Olympics in 2012 proved a very useful inspiration.'

1 July 2016
Brian Adcock
Independent

Michael Gove said his bid to become prime minister was driven by 'conviction' about what was right for the country rather than personal ambition. He said that when he concluded Boris Johnson was not 'the right person', his 'heart told him' to put himself forward: 'I did almost everything not to be a candidate for the leadership of this party. I was so very reluctant because I know my limitations. Whatever charisma is, I don't have it, whatever glamour may be, I don't think anyone could ever associate me with it.' Meanwhile, Welsh football fans hailed their team's 3-1 win against Belgium as the country's greatest ever victory, securing a place in their first ever major tournament semi-final.

3 July 2016
Bob Moran
Daily Telegraph

Nigel Farage announced his resignation as UKIP leader, stating that he 'couldn't possibly achieve more' and adding, 'I want my life back.' The heavy-drinking and smoking MEP was accused of cowardice for leaving front-line politics rather than helping to sort out Britain's exit from the European Union.

5 July 2016
Dave Brown
Independent

6 July 2016
Christian Adams
Daily Telegraph

The Chilcot Inquiry found that Tony Blair had overstated the threat posed by Saddam Hussein, sent ill-prepared troops to Iraq and had 'wholly inadequate' plans for the aftermath of the invasion. Sir John Chilcot determined that the 2003 invasion was not, in fact, the 'last resort' presented to MPs and the public. There was no 'imminent threat' from Saddam and the intelligence case was 'not justified', he said. Blair apologised for any mistakes he had made, but not for the decision to go to war.

Michael Gove's betrayal of Boris Johnson was understood to be the reason for his failure to make the final round of the Tory leadership contest. Supporters of the former justice secretary said his decision to unexpectedly withdraw his backing for the former London mayor, causing Johnson to pull out of the race, had infuriated his fellow MPs. Gove dropped out of the race himself, after winning the support of just 46 of the 330 Tory MPs.

8 July 2016
Peter Brookes
The Times

10 July 2016
Bob Moran
Daily Telegraph

Andrea Leadsom suggested in an interview with *The Times* that being a mother made her a better choice than Theresa May to succeed David Cameron as prime minister, as it showed that she had 'a very real stake' in the future of the country. The comments, made just a few days after May spoke about her inability to have children with her husband, sparked a huge backlash, with some Tories questioning her suitability to be prime minister. Leadsom accused the newspaper of 'gutter journalism' and demanded a retraction. Just two days later, she resigned from the leadership race.

According to the cartoonist: 'This cartoon was produced during Wimbledon, hence the tennis metaphor. After a large number of Labour MPs had resigned from the shadow cabinet in protest at Jeremy Corbyn's leadership, Angela Eagle was planning to take him on in a leadership battle. Yet with Corbyn's massive support from grassroots groups in the Labour membership such as Momentum, it seemed that Eagle's attempt would be completely futile. So I depicted her as about to serve against Corbyn yet, with all his backers, the match is already won.'

10 July 2016
Ben Jennings
Guardian

On David Cameron's final day as prime minister, a removal van pulled into Downing Street, while ministers gathered to pay tribute to Cameron in his 215th, and final, cabinet meeting. Cameron, irritated at Steve Bell's portrayal of him, had told Bell at the 2010 Tory party conference that 'You can only push the condom so far.' At his last Prime Minister's Question Time, Cameron enjoyed a final bittersweet moment in the limelight as he told the Commons, 'I was the future, once' – Bell's cartoon, drawn the previous day, had coincidentally included the same words.

13 July 2016
Steve Bell
Guardian

Boris Johnson thought his front-line political career was finished after his failure to stand for the Tory leadership contest. However, a source close to Theresa May said Johnson still had the new prime minister's respect: 'He is a senior member of our party and should be treated as such. And she does like him.' To everyone's surprise, May made Johnson foreign secretary in her cabinet.

14 July 2016
Christian Adams
Daily Telegraph

15 July 2016
Ian Knox
Irish News

Theresa Villiers resigned as Northern Ireland secretary, adding that the 'new prime minister was kind enough to offer me a role but it was not one which I felt I could take on'. James Brokenshire, an ally of the new prime minister, replaced her. According to the cartoonist: 'Until Theresa Villiers came out as a rabid brexiteer she was seen as a peripheral hands-off minister. One of our trade-union leaders, "Bumper" Graham, compared her to Cruella de Vil from *One Hundred and One Dalmatians*.'

Eighty-four people, including many children, were murdered when a lorry drove through a crowd celebrating Bastille Day in the French city of Nice. The driver, an ISIS sympathiser, continued for over a mile on the Promenade des Anglais before being shot dead by police. French president François Hollande said the attack was of 'an undeniable terrorist nature'.

16 July 2016
Bob Moran
Daily Telegraph

Whose Coup is it Anyway?

According to the cartoonist: 'Hot on the heels of the attempted coup in Turkey, Jeremy Corbyn faced a Labour leadership coup from Angela Eagle. Then Owen Smith threw his hat into the ring, arguing that there should only be one opponent standing against their beleaguered leader. Eagle disagreed, stating that "politics is not about taking sides". It ended amicably the next day when Eagle stepped down, saying that she and Smith were in "lockstep" together, suggesting some agreement had been made between them.'

18 July 2016
Chris Duggan
The Times

'There she goes... One unarmed torpedo, round the coast, down the Thames, into the drains, then straight up Jeremy Corbyn's lavatory.'

MPs voted to renew the Trident nuclear programme after Theresa May told them it would be 'an act of gross irresponsibility' for the UK to abandon its nuclear weapons. The prime minister accused critics of Trident of being 'the first to defend the country's enemies'. Jeremy Corbyn, who voted against the government, warned of the effect that using an 'indiscriminate weapon of mass destruction' could have. He received much criticism from his own backbenchers who reminded him that Labour's official policy was in favour of renewal.

19 July 2016
Stan McMurtry
Daily Mail

Theresa May likened Jeremy Corbyn to 'an unscrupulous boss' as she made her debut in Prime Minister's Question Time . As the two leaders clashed on workers' rights, the prime minister said: 'I suspect there are many members on the Opposition benches who might be familiar with an unscrupulous boss; a boss who doesn't listen to his workers; a boss who requires some of his workers to double their workload; and maybe even a boss who exploits the rules to further his own career.' Leaning forward and fixing Corbyn with a direct stare, she added: 'Remind him of anybody?'

21 July 2016
Peter Brookes
The Times

Bathed in the Bile of the I Am

Accepting the Republican nomination in Cleveland, Ohio, Donald Trump pledged to be a voice for working Americans, to restore law and order and to confound doubters by winning the White House. 'Nobody knows the system better than me, which is why I alone can fix it . . . My message is that things have to change and they have to change right now.' Guardian columnist Jonathan Freedland thought 'Teleprompter Trump was charmless, deprived of the spontaneity and humour that made him a compelling candidate.'

23 July 2016
Martin Rowson
Guardian

REFORMING THE UNACCEPTABLE FACE OF CAPITALISM...

26 July 2016
Dave Brown
Independent

Theresa May faced calls to get tough on irresponsible business practices by stripping the former BHS boss Sir Philip Green of his knighthood. A report from a group of MPs described how Green made millions of pounds for himself and his wife, leaving the chain store on 'life support' before selling it off to a 'wholly unsuitable chancer'. A spokeswoman for the prime minister said the government planned to take action, after a damning report by MPs into the collapse of the retailer concluded that it had fallen prey to the 'unacceptable face of capitalism'.

Owen Smith's challenge against Jeremy Corbyn for the Labour leadership was set to continue until the Labour party conference on 24 September. Meanwhile, *Harry Potter and the Cursed Child* opened in London on 30 July – the play is in two parts and lasts more than five hours.

26 July 2016
Christian Adams
Daily Telegraph

Donald Trump selected Indiana Governor Mike Pence as his presidential running mate hoping that Pence, a former congressman popular among social conservatives, could help him shore up support among wavering Republicans. Trump and Putin had seemed to voice support for each other on several occasions, leading critics of the Republican nominee to accuse the American of having similarly dictatorial aspirations. On social media many people branded Trump a 'Siberian Candidate', a reference to the 1959 thriller *The Manchurian Candidate*, in which the Soviets plot to use a brainwashed Korean War veteran in a coup in America.

30 July 2016
Kevin Kallaugher
The Economist

HOUSE OF LORDS OPENING CEREMONY...

David Cameron rewarded his political allies in his final honours list as prime minister, as even his wife's stylist Isabel Spearman received an OBE for political and public service. Katie Ghose, the chief executive of the Electoral Reform Society, denounced the list, saying: 'For a prime minister who promised to cut the cost of politics, David Cameron is leaving a big bill for the taxpayer as he leaves office. His parting gift of 16 lords is a sorry legacy, both in terms of cost to the taxpayer and the quality of our democracy. These unelected peers will cost the taxpayer millions over the long-term – hardly a fitting goodbye.'

6 August 2016
Morten Morland
The Times

10 August 2016
Dave Brown
Independent

One hundred and thirty thousand Labour party members, including Steve Bell, were excluded from voting in the leadership election when the party's National Executive Committee ruled that full members could only vote if they had at least six months' continuous membership. Lawyers representing a group of five members claimed their clients had been unfairly excluded from participating. Justice Hickinbottom found in favour of the new party members, stating that their exclusion was a breach of contract.

Donald Trump sparked anger at a rally in North Carolina by appearing to suggest that his supporters could stop Hillary Clinton by exercising their right to bear arms. In response to a huge backlash, he asserted that he had merely been urging gun-rights supporters to vote in large numbers. However, House Speaker Paul Ryan, the highest-ranked elected Republican, called it an inappropriate joke.

11 August 2016
Christian Adams
Daily Telegraph

Jeremy Corbyn dismissed claims by Labour deputy leader Tom Watson that hard-left activists were trying to infiltrate the Labour party ahead of the leadership vote. Corbyn said Watson's suggestion that 'Trotsky entryists' were manipulating younger party members to boost his support was 'nonsense'. Watson responded by saying there was 'clear and incontrovertible evidence that a small group of Trotskyite activists have taken leading roles in the Labour party or are seeking to do so'.

13 August 2016
Ben Jennings
i

Trade Secretary Liam Fox was branded 'nutty and obsessive' by government insiders, as his battle with Boris Johnson over Brexit escalated. A leaked letter revealed a conflict between the pair, leading a source at the Foreign Office to say about Fox, 'There's something strange about him.' The source also claimed that Fox and the Minister for Brexit David Davis had a 'much more extreme point of view' than Johnson on Europe, and called their opinion 'simplistic'. The comments came after Theresa May had warned the trio against government in-fighting.

17 August 2016
Morten Morland
The Times

18 August 2016
Martin Rowson
Guardian

Owen Smith was put under pressure to explain controversial comments suggesting that there should be negotiations with ISIS to end the civil war in Syria. As he was attacked by both Tory and Labour politicians, a spokesman said: 'Owen is clear that there should be absolutely no negotiation with Daesh, or any terrorist group, until they renounce violence, cease all acts of terror and commit themselves to a peaceful settlement.'

It's the perfect recipe for growth!

Theresa May abandoned plans to tackle childhood obesity by curbing junk food advertising, and instead challenged supermarkets and manufacturers to cut the amount of sugar in their products by a fifth. Ministers were accused of a 'shocking abdication of responsibility' and heavily criticised by doctors and dentists for watering down the strategy to prevent childhood obesity.

19 August 2016
Morten Morland
The Times

In an uncharacteristic move aimed at kick-starting his struggling presidential campaign, Donald Trump admitted for the first time that he regretted some of his outrageous comments. Reading from an autocue, Trump said: 'Sometimes in the heat of debate and speaking on a multitude of issues, you don't choose the right words or you say the wrong thing. I have done that, and believe it or not, I regret it – and I do regret it – particularly where it may have caused personal pain.' It was a rare admission from a man who had said that he prefers 'not to regret anything'.

20 August 2016
Bob Moran
Daily Telegraph

Jeremy Corbyn reacted angrily to questions about his spat with Sir Richard Branson. The Virgin Trains tycoon had challenged Corbyn's claim that he could not find a seat on a 'jam-packed' train. Corbyn tried to ignore questions about it at a tetchy press conference, saying he had been searching for two seats next to each other. At a press conference held to talk about his policies for the NHS, he said sarcastically: 'I am very pleased that Richard Branson has been able to break off from his holiday to take this issue seriously and with the importance it obviously deserves.'

25 August 2016
Christian Adams
Daily Telegraph

The French prime minister Manuel Valls defended a ban on burkinis, saying that the full-body swimsuit symbolised the enslavement of women. Photographs of armed police ordering a Muslim woman on a beach in Nice to partially disrobe caused global consternation. According to the cartoonist: 'This idea came to me after quite a long struggle. The sight of police officers standing over Muslim women on French beaches, asking them to remove their clothes was already ridiculous, laughable. They pushed the subject beyond satire. How could a cartoon possibly top that?'

28 August 2016
Peter Schrank
Sunday Business Post

With Theresa May having cited Queen Elizabeth I as a role model, Labour MP Barry Gardiner proposed a more negative comparison. Complaining about the prime minister's plan to trigger Article 50 without a new parliamentary vote on the subject, Gardiner accused May of acting 'to diminish parliament and assume the arrogant powers of a Tudor monarch'.

29 August 2016
Martin Rowson
Guardian

30 August 2016
Brian Adcock
Independent

According to the cartoonist: 'In his autobiography, the ever-so-dignified former shadow chancellor Ed Balls had been slagging off Jeremy Corbyn's leadership style, calling it a "leftist utopian fantasy". This came just a few days before Mr Balls was to indulge in his own fantasy by dancing his heart out and attempting to win *Strictly Come Dancing*.'

Theresa May ruled out calling an early UK general election to take advantage of the Conservatives' huge lead over Labour in the opinion polls, and confirmed there would be no parliamentary vote on Brexit. Meanwhile, the actor Gene Wilder, who played Leo Bloom in *The Producers*, died aged 83.

31 August 2016
Peter Brookes
The Times